The Art and Science of
Tesla Teaching
The 7 Keys to Training Like Nikola
By: Max Kopsho

Tesla Teaching

The Art and Science of
Tesla Teaching
The 7 Keys to Training Like Nikola
By: Max Kopsho

"Tesla Teaching" was written for the Audiovisual industry but it is great for trainers and communicators (everyone for that matter) in every industry. IF you are looking for a book that just gives you some simple yet powerful advice on how to improve your presentation and communication skills you found it, this book in its entirety covers much more.

There are so many training and communications books out there and many books out there about Nikola Tesla. Most of the books about Nikola Tesla are about the controversial things he did near the end of his life and there are not nearly enough books about the wondrous inventions or incredible works he accomplished. From what I can tell not a single book out there is about Nikola Tesla AND training. This book is all about developing the attributes that made Nikola the great Training Guru (and communicator) that many may not recognize him as being.

Nikola Tesla was one of the key founders of modern technology (including AV.) He also transferred his love for communication and science into the business of training. In his communications, he used demonstrations that were incredibly convincing to teach people how safe alternating current was. As engineer and inventor there is no question, he was incredibly successful. This book explores how you can apply the training principles developed by one of the most brilliant and creative minds in history.

Read this book to discover what it takes to blend art and science to provide unique training and communication approaches for your customers. Can you train like Nikola?

3

Tesla Teaching

Tesla Teaching was edited by Christine Kopsho

An Important Note: This book was edited by my wife Christine. She is a four-time cancer victor. Without the wonderful medical team that saved her, The Leukemia and Lymphoma Society (LLS) and Be the Match she would not be here today. If you learn nothing else from this book, please learn that a bone marrow transplant can save a life (like it did for Christine.) Christine received her bone marrow donation from an unmatched and unrelated donor straight off the Be the Match registry. The registration process is an easy cheek swab. Many people on the recipient waiting list are simply waiting for you to go through a simple registration and infusion process so they can use your life saving stem cells. Saving a life does not have to be painful or expensive. Saving a life simply takes a small first step. Consider registering today at www.bethematch.org, you might save someone's best friend, lifelong companion, mother of four and all-around great person. Also, consider donating to The Leukemia & Lymphoma Society at www.lls.org. LLS is the largest voluntary cancer research agency specifically focused on finding cures and better treatments for blood cancer patients. Blood cancers are part of a group of "orphan diseases" with small markets and limited profit potential which means very little funding from the large pharmaceutical companies and trending support organizations. Every year over 160,000 people who are newly diagnosed with blood cancer now count on people like you to help find a cure.

In this same spirit, 50% of the profits from the sales of this book will be donated to the Leukemia and Lymphoma Society in honor of Christine Kopsho.

www.bethematch.org,

The Art and Science of

Tesla Teaching

The 7 Keys to Training Like Nikola

By: Max Kopsho

Tesla Teaching

This publication is designed to provide accurate and authoritative information regarding the subject matter covered. It is sold with the understanding that the publisher is not engaged in rendering legal, accounting, or other professional service. If legal advice or other expert assistance is required, the service of a competent professional person should be sought.

ISBN: 978-0-692-75262-3

Library of Congress Control Number: 2016910946

This book is currently registered with AVIXA's RU Provider Program with grAVITation TECHnologies as the RU provider for 2 CTS RUs, or 2 CTS-D RUs, or 2 CTS-I RUs or a combination thereof totaling 2 RUs.

AVIXA

CTS RU Provider

Once you have read the book you can claim your RUs at www.gravitationtech.com/tesla-quiz

Table of Contents

Why This book? Why Now?

In the technology industry (the AV industry specifically) we must grow our own successors and training is vital to that end. We often find ourselves challenged with using trainers that we borrow from other divisions in our organizations to close the gap. Whether we use senior technical people to train our new sales staff or advanced sales engineers to train the new techs the result is usually the same. We put these new trainers in a position where they are doing their best to transfer their knowledge to the others. They do not do as well as expected because they have not been formally trained in the art and science of training and communication. Of course, they don't do as well as expected. They have not been through the programs that spend years on teaching and mentoring trainers on how to transfer their knowledge, skill, and attitude to bring out the full potential in their students.

There are many training and communications books out there and many books out there about Nikola Tesla. Most of the books about Nikola Tesla are about the controversial activities and projects near the end of his life. From what I can tell, there is not a single book out there about Nikola Tesla AND training. This book is all about developing the key principles that made Nikola Tesla the great communicator and technical trainer that few people know that he was.

Did you know that Nikola Tesla was one of the key founders of AV technology (AC Power, Radio, and Control)? Did you know he also transferred his love for art and science into the business of technology communications? As chief electrical engineer, inventor, and product manager, there is no question he was incredibly successful. But he was also undeniably successful in applying his knowledge and skills in technology training. Learn from Tesla's successes and failures as seen through the eyes of the technology training segment.

Tesla Teaching

Examine the principles that were used in early technological communication and training from of one of the first and best to use them. Read this book to discover what it takes to blend art and science to bring out the potential in your students in all your training and communication endeavors.

The *7 Keys* outlined in this book and are as follows:

Capability – Train from a Place of Authority/Knowledge
Competence – Solid, Proven, and Memorable Training
Cleverness – Teach in New Ways to Match Learners
Curiosity – Be Like Your Learners, Always Ask Why
Commitment – Teach in Accordance with Your Purpose
Confidence – Have an Attitude That Attendees Wants
Controversy – Make Attendees Want to Act

BONUS Chapter - **Creativity**: Max's Training Tips & Tricks.

Follow the guidelines in this book and you will learn the keys to engaging your audiences and bringing out their maximum potential through facilitation and information and experiential sharing. I truly hope you enjoy this read as you learn how to master the art and science of Tesla Teaching. Read this book to learn to sell train and communicate technology like Nikola.

A lot of what you read in this book may be a reminder of what you already know about communicating technology. I believe that we all need to be reminded of what got us where we are. Sometimes we need to do a little refocusing and get a bump back in the right direction. Sometimes we need this type of catalyst so that we can move to the next level or get back where we should be. I wrote this book to share things that I know and things I work on regularly to improve on in my own technology training career. It is a constant cycle of learning, applying, relearning, and reapplying.

Tesla Teaching

Dedication

To my late mother: Thank you for teaching me the importance of balance in life. Where dad taught me technology and art, you taught me passion, emotion, and communication.

I dedicate this book to my late mother – Charlene Eloise Kopsho. Like Tesla, even though we both lost our mothers early in life, we both attribute much of our intelligence and ingenuity to our mothers. I will never achieve the level of intelligence or ingenuity that Nickola had and moreover I can never give justice to the levels of intelligence and ingenuity that my mother tried to impart on me, but if even a little came across, I am a very lucky man. My mom was one of the most intelligent people I have ever known. She lived in a time when it was expected that she would stay home and raise the kids and know her place. But that never stopped her from learning and keeping up to date on the need-to-know goings on in the world. My mom could finish the New York Times crossword puzzle in a matter of minutes (usually because that is all the time she had while raising the six of us, including one child with extremely challenging special needs.) My mother sacrificed all of her creature comforts so that we could feel that we had it all. Growing up we felt like we were all princes and one princess. Due to the love, hard work, and sacrifices of my mother, we never felt alone, unloved, and we never even missed a meal. From her I learned the art of communication and how to read people. I learned how to take the time to be compassionate, sympathetic, and often empathetic. I was supposed to be raised Catholic, but my mother died when I was rather young. When I finally converted to Catholicism. I chose my confirmation name to be Gabriel. This was due to the communication nature that my mother instilled in me so many years before and that has followed me in my career as a trainer and presenter to this day, so many years later. That balance of technology and communication is what makes me a Tesla Teacher just like my mom   was.

Tesla Teaching

Charlene Eloise Kopsho.
(1936-1983)
My Tesla Teacher
Mom, I love you!

Tesla Teaching

PREFACE

Preface - Tesla the Communicator

Knowledge – Skill - Attitude

"Invention is the most important product of man's creative brain. The ultimate purpose is the complete mastery of mind over the material world, the harnessing of human nature to human needs. My Inventions, in Electrical Experimenter magazine (1919)"

– Nikola Tesla –
*The Wonder World To Be Created By Electricity,
Manufacturer's Record, September 9, 1915*

Preface Section 1

This book is divided into three parts. Knowledge, Skill and Attitude. Tesla was able to balance these three major attributes to form his technology communication abilities.

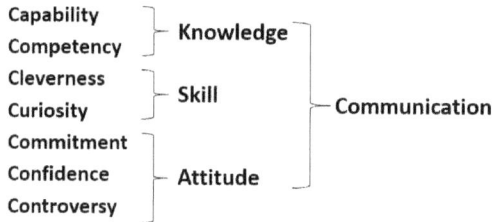

Figure 1

The beauty in Tesla's contributions to the scientific community and the second industrial revolution are in his way of communicating more than his inventions. He shared more information and more insights than anything. It was learned after his death that many "inventors" stole much of their research and their inventions were based on information that they received from Tesla himself in presentations and lectures.

Oddly, much of the books and articles that have been written about Tesla did not mention the kind of communicator Tesla was. Most authors like to focus on the controversy and his inventions. One book does stand out though. Margaret Cheney does very eloquently describe the type of speaker and trainer that Tesla was. I could base a lot of the structure of this book on her findings and then use my other research about Tesla to support her description of his training and presentation techniques.

Tesla Teaching

Here is an excerpt from *Tesla – Man Out of Time*, by Margaret Cheney that gives us a better appreciation for the amazing technology communicator Nikola Tesla was: ..." The audience, riveted by the cadence flow of words, the play of lights and magic, would stare as in a trance.

The language of science then being completely inadequate, Tesla described visual effects in the style of a poet in love with the sheer dance of flame and light. Indeed, it seemed as if these were as significant to him as tapping the energy within."

My read of the way Margaret describes the way Tesla presents and the way his audience reacts and is completely consumed by his communication skills is more telling than the content contained in his presentation.

So why am I writing this book about training and presentation/communication skills using Tesla? Why am I using a person from history that is not known for his communication skills? Well, like I did in Da Vinci Sales – The Seven Keys to Selling Like Leonardo, my goal is for us to find the characteristics in this amazing historical figure that many missed and see that we have these same attributes and we are possibly just overlooking those as well. It also helps that, like in Da Vinci Sales, we are using a pioneer in AV/IT just like we are now with Tesla.

How is it that I see a trainer in Tesla and almost no other historian or author sees this? I think it is important I answer this question before we go into the seven keys to teaching like Nikola. My first justification for this classification is whether we like it or not we all tend to keep some of our characteristics of our parents and to me this holds true for Nikola. Nikola was the son of a Serbian Orthodox Reverend. By the nature of their trade and conviction a reverend is a teacher. I absolutely believe some of these traits had to rub off on Nikola.

Another reason that I believe that Nikola Tesla was destined to be identified as a teacher, presenter, and communicator as much as inventor and genius was that his mother was a hard-working woman of many talents who created appliances to help with home and farm responsibilities. One of these was a mechanical eggbeater. Cool! An invention based on need. Tesla attributed all his inventive instincts to his mother. I see this as a sign of her ability to teach her ways to him and in that he would clearly learn ways to teach as well. In the best situations, we are products of our upbringing, there is no denying that we ultimately become the best of what each of our parents have to offer. Nikola is no exception. His mother plays the role of the teacher, innovator and genius at home and his father being known as the "Man of Justice" (his Nom De Plume). Another example of Nikola coming from a background of communicators is that his father was an Orthodox Priest (they are the ones who can marry and have families). Nikola was destined to be both technologist and communicator.

Preface Section 2

In this section of the Preface I would also like to address communication in general. I could not make this stream of consciousness fit into any of the chapters in the book, so I decided to add a second section to the preface.

Every interaction with other people is a form of presentation. It may be a simple one-to-one spontaneous water cooler discussion or a fully choreographed event. While we may use the term "presentation" this often represents just a one-way discussion… and while it may be semantics, it must be about "communication" not just presentation.

To talk about presentations and the way we envision they should be, we should talk about the experience. Presentations must go beyond one directional information flow and PowerPoint. Presentations should be an experience. That is why we talk about the "Evolution of True Communication."

The Evolution of True Communication is that sweet spot where three basic categories of presentations come together: the technology and tools, the environment and space planning, and the presentation and the presenter.

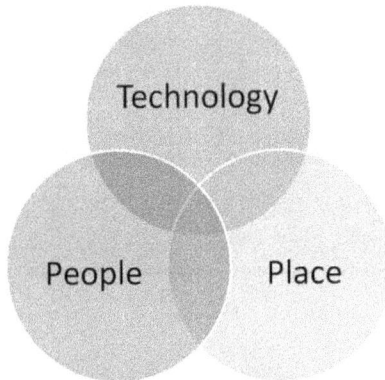

Figure 2

When all three come together you will find that you have a dynamic and knowledgeable presenter using great materials given in an optimal environment enhanced by the most applicable technical tools available. This all forms one cohesive experience for the observer/participant that fully draws them in and commits them to content and causes them to invest as many senses, emotions, thoughts as possible. The goal of The Evolution of True Communication is to have the observer/participant become part of the presentation.

The Evolution of True Communication is completely dependent on the communication model. This is to say that the success of The Evolution of True Communication hinges on how well information is relayed. To close the loop on this discussion it may help to agree on a way of explaining the communication model. For this we have come up with the 7 Cs of the Hierarchy of Communication.

The 7 C's of the Hierarchy of Communications:

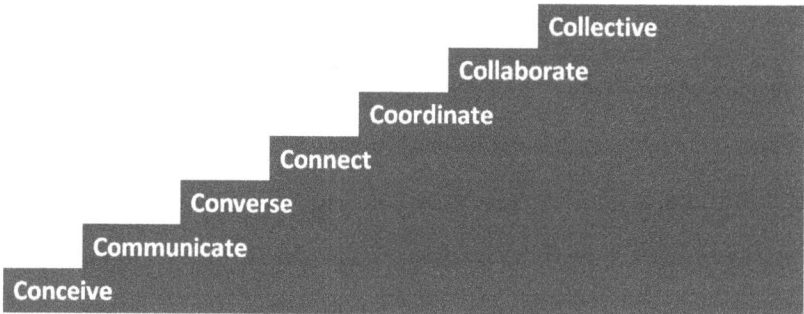

Figure 3

Tesla Teaching

1. **Conceive** – The lowest level of the Presentation, where the presenter has merely conceived an idea. The idea is a thought and may even be records but is not shared.

2. **Communicate** – The second step in The Evolution of True Communication is where the presenter is now able to share the thought but is in strict "presentation" mode. This is when the presentation is one-way communication. PowerPoint is a good example of the second step in this hierarchy. The presenter can share the thought but is not very good at turning the concept into a two-way conversation.

3. **Converse** – This third step in the hierarchy of The Evolution of True Communication elevates the presenter to a facilitator and allows the audience to share their ideas as well. Now the presentation turns into a conversation and some discussion is allowed.

4. **Connect** – The fourth level in The Evolution of True Communication is when emotion and senses are included and there is a true connection made. The presenter is elevated to educator or mentor and the audience is invested. This is still a conversation of sorts, but everyone is a stakeholder.

5. **Coordinate** – The fifth step in the chain is close to the fourth. At this point in The Evolution of True Communication, the presenter and audience are still connected and sharing but their information flow is better facilitated and tends to have a solid and unified flow and direction.

6. **Collaborate** – This sixth and key step to The Evolution of True Communication allows for every person in the environment to have an equal "sitting." Everyone is both the presenter and audience at the same time. Information is shared and documented in one unified location.

7. **Collective** – The seventh and final place in The Evolution of True Communication is when all are of one thought. This place in the hierarchy is utopian and somewhat impossible. Think of this as the socialism of meeting environments, where the concept is nice, but could never work in practicality.

Tesla Teaching

As you progress through the hierarchy of communication in The Evolution of True Communication you also grow from being dependent to independent and then to interdependent. This is a beautiful illustration of the same type of growth explained in Stephen Covey's Seven Habits of Highly Effective People.

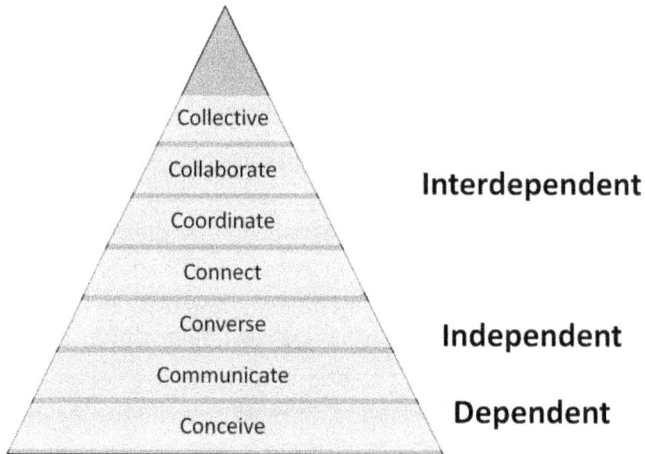

Figure 4

When we look at the Hierarchy of Communication, we note that it isn't necessary to have every meeting or presentation hit all the way to level 6 of The Hierarchy of Communications. Some meetings are just presentations for information dissemination. When you need to have a meeting where The Hierarchy of Communications (Level 6) communication happens, what key elements do you have to have?

As indicated earlier, to obtain The Hierarchy of Communications at Level 6 you need the three following things:

1. Technology
2. Place
3. People

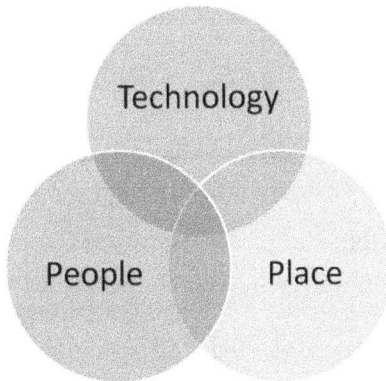

Figure 5

Technology – The use of training and presentation technology and tool can truly enhance communication. It can also cripple a presentation. When using technology and tools for The Evolution of True Communication it is vital that the tools SUPPORT the message. The available technology should help to relay the message. For example: the use of audiovisual integration by placing document cameras in the ceiling then using video processors that can support the ability to "slide" a document across the table so that remote participants can see the documents in their room AND can edit and collaborate on these documents using the network. Using these technologies and tools instantly elevates a typical presentation to The Hierarchy of Communications at Level 6. This is more than just BYOD (bring-your-own-device) and a "share button" with an original equipment manufacturer (OEM, or off the shelf) PC. This requires additional design and integration in space planning and training for the presenter on how to best use the materials.

If we wanted to breakdown *some* of the categories of technologies and tools that could be used to help create The Evolution of True Communication, the list could contain:

- Acoustics
- AV over Networks
- Collaboration Systems
- Cameras / Visualizers
- Control System or
    iPad/Tablet Control
- Displays
- Encoders/Decoders
- Interactive Whiteboards
    and Displays
- Lighting
- Loudspeakers
	- Moving from the Phone
	    Call to Desktop
	    Conferencing to Room
	    Conferencing
	- Recording /Archiving
	- Sound Masking
	- Streaming/Online Multicast
	- Unified Communications &
	    Collaboration
	- Video Processors
	- Videoconferencing
	- Voting/Polling System

Figure 6

Tesla Teaching

Place – Place is a combination of Environment and Space Planning. When we add this to the way we build a presentation space to support The Evolution of True Communication we are enhancing the way people communicate by making them more comfortable using physics. For in-room meetings we improve the acoustics, lighting, human factors, and furnishings to eliminate distractions and barriers to communications. We can also make the space adapt to the types of meetings that take place by planning for multipurpose usability. Space planning and environment design accounts for local collaborative impact and communication in different environments such as seated or standing meetings or small group collaborative or one-way large audience meetings.

Space planning is used to create a natural environment for videoconferencing with proper audiovisual integration that includes proper lighting, acoustics, camera, microphone, loudspeaker placement and display sizing and placement. These things can give the users the feeling that the remote participants are in the room. There is a science to getting the placement and sizing right to make the system feel natural and fit in the environment. Audiovisual system designers and engineers' study this and do an incredible amount of research (and questioning) before making recommendations about how to deploy a system.

I also cannot underestimate the importance of the trainer/teacher being one hundred percent in charge of their environment (space). This is to say that the temperature, room layout, location (with respect to break area and facilities), and other environment/space factors are the trainer's/teacher's responsibilities. If you are a contract trainer and travel around for your sessions, this needs to be added to your contract. You must have access to temperature controls; you must be the one to determine location of the room, and so on.

Tesla Teaching

People – While we used People as the heading, it is really a combination of the actual Presentation as well as the Presenter and the capabilities. We have a mnemonic we use to help prepare presenters for an event that may help to illustrate some of the needed items for a presenter and the presentation. That mnemonic is SMILE.

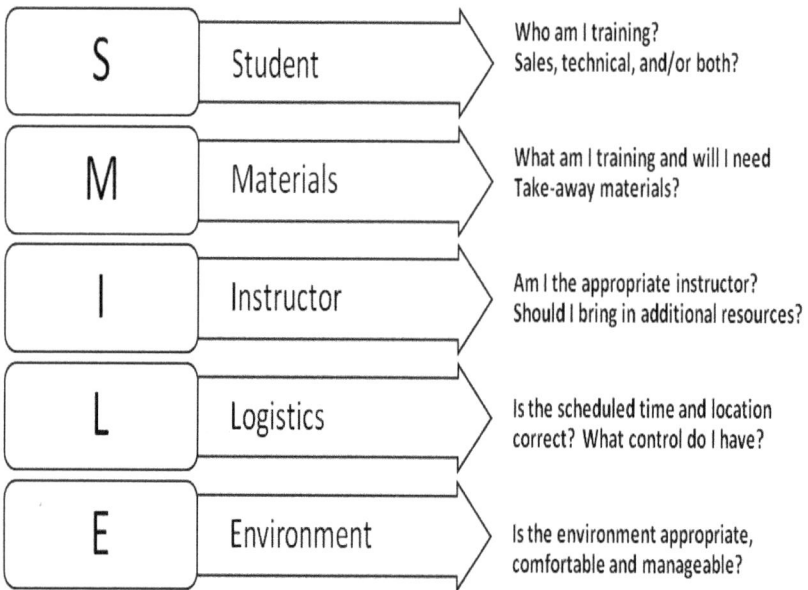

S	Student	Who am I training? Sales, technical, and/or both?
M	Materials	What am I training and will I need Take-away materials?
I	Instructor	Am I the appropriate instructor? Should I bring in additional resources?
L	Logistics	Is the scheduled time and location correct? What control do I have?
E	Environment	Is the environment appropriate, comfortable and manageable?

Figure 7

In Chapter 3, I refer to this as the "You Factor." The "You Factor" is the realization that the value comes when the combination of the presenter, the space, and the technology (the system) are blended for maximum impact. All too often we, as presenters, become too dependent on the system and the content to be the crux of the message.

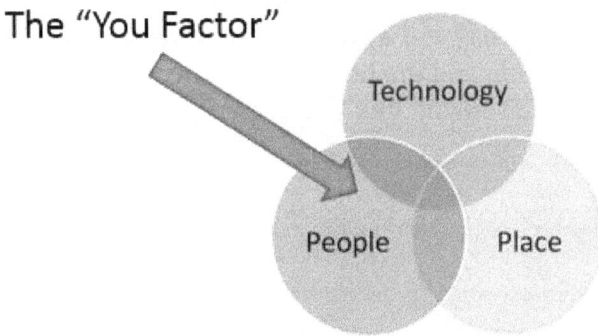

Figure 8

The emphasis here is on your ability to tie all of this together and add your value. The most important element of getting the most of your presentation system and to obtain The Evolution of True Communication is making sure that you consider the presenter and presentation materials as part of the system. The presenter is the most important part of The Evolution of True Communication. It is important to consult with, train, and keep an ongoing partnership with customers to ensure that they are the best presenters they can be; that they are fully equipped to utilize the highly optimized technical tools that are specified and designed into a system. Make sure they are completely comfortable in the enhanced spaces that have been built and support them as a cohesive team.

Tesla Teaching

The Evolution of True Communication is so much more than attending or hosting a meeting where information is provided TO the audience in a "death by PowerPoint" fashion. When you have successfully achieved The Evolution of True Communication, audience and presenters alike are involved in the creation, sharing, management, manipulation, ownership and the care of the content and everyone is better for it. In the Evolution of True Communication, presenters become mentors, the audience becomes collaborators, and everyone can add value to the message. This is all accomplished because the best tools and technology are available, the environment is optimal for the application and the presenter and materials are perfectly matched. When all of this aligns perfectly, it is a beautiful thing.

CHAPTER 1

Capability

Training From a Place of Authority and Knowledge.
Providing Training that is Informative and Valuable.

(Know Your Audience and Their Education Needs)

"It is paradoxical, yet true, to say, that the more we know, the more ignorant we become in the absolute sense, for it is only through enlightenment that we become conscious of our limitations. Precisely one of the most gratifying results of intellectual evolution is the continuous opening up of new and greater prospects."
– Nikola Tesla –
The Wonder World to Be Created by Electricity,
Manufacturer's Record, September 9, 1915

Tesla Teaching

Tesla Example – Although very much a self-taught life-long learner, Nikola was highly respected and even the most skeptical scientists could not find fault in his findings. "Despite the fireworks, philosophy, and poetry, his every scientific claim was based on experiments he personally repeated at least twenty times." – The Stage – The Lights (Fifty Years) – "…Yet no scientist could fault him on technical details." Quoted from Nikola Tesla Man Out of Time by Margaret Chaney.

The Lesson - Training from a place of authority/knowledge research is key. I have learned that the research is the most valuable part of the training for the presenter and the audience. It only makes sense that the more comfortable you are with the material. the more freedom you must be yourself while presenting.

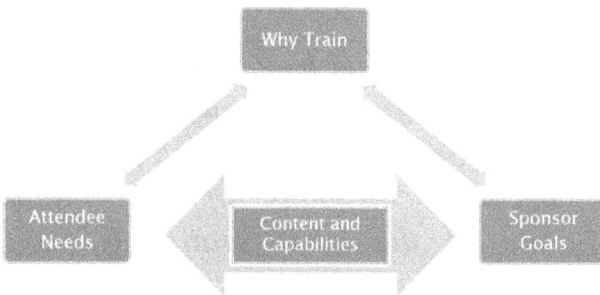

Figure 9

Does the content meet the sponsor's goals, and can I close skills and experience the gap?

The major aspects of your research should be something like the following:

-Research the reason for the training. Knowing this helps with the attitude and builds on your commitment and purpose (chapter 5).

Tesla Teaching

-Research the goals of the training. If you are the sponsor of the session, this should be easy. If not, it is best to find out what is the expected outcome directly from the sponsors or hosts of the training.

-Research the average attendee and their needs. Are the attendee's needs and the sponsor need completely aligned? If not, how far apart are they and can you quickly do an assessment to see if the training can meet the goals of the sponsor and the attendee?

-This may not be research, but you also need to make sure that your knowledge, skill, and experience match the needs of the sponsor, attendees, and the content. Once you have done the full gap analysis to determine where the gaps are between what the sponsor goals and attendee goals are and what you can do and you determine you can leap that gap, then you can continue. This may sound silly, but it is a simple rule of finding out the simple: "WHY are we doing this training?"

Once you have matched the goals/needs and the training resources, it is time to take a deeper look at the content. The key determination here is to see if a proper lesson plan has been developed or not. In my experience, this is an area that is most often missed (especially in the corporate world). I would estimate that over 90% of the trainings I have attended there was clearly no lesson plan. Most trainings are conducted because someone developed them directly into the presentation (PowerPoint). I liken this to building the plane while you are flying it. While you are focused on staying in the air and using all of your resources to do so (building slides that follow a stream of consciousness), you are neglecting the navigation and landing systems (outline and closing point). When you work from the presentation mindset it is too easy to focus on the message while it is being said instead of the "close." The landing and navigation are missing. This is where a lesson plan comes into play.

Tesla Teaching

A proper lesson plan will contain the following at a minimum:

- A Complete Course Outline
- Clearly Stated Training Goals (Chapter 2)
  - Target Learning Objectives
  - Single Minded Propositions
- Clearly Stated Metrics for Success
- Clearly Defined Timelines

Every training engagement should be looked at as a new job or project that may require resources that you or your organization may not currently possess. In my book Da Vinci Sales, I refer to Hope is Not a Strategy – The Six Keys to the Complex Sale by Rick Paige. In this reference, I discuss his "RADAR" approach to account management (Reading Accounts and Deploying Appropriate Resources). The same "RADAR" approach should be used for training. As a training manager for many of the places I worked, I have done many of the trainings myself but there were also many times when I looked at the gap between the goals of the training and the needs of the attendees and determined that the gap required knowledge and/or skill beyond my own. At that time, I became the training project manager. Being a project manager of training made me move from being the person who conducted the training to being the person who deployed the appropriate resources.

If you are the sponsor, my personal advice is to always attend the trainings that you schedule and orchestrate when possible. I have made the conscious decision to be a life-long learner and that has served me very well. That is one of my Tesla Training attributes. One of my biggest pet-peeves is when managers and sponsors do not attend trainings that they arrange or sponsor. The importance of the training diminishes considerably if they do not assign enough value to attend it themselves.

Tesla Teaching

To speak from authority and knowledge, I have found that this authority can be borrowed or recently obtained and researched. For example, "this content is compiled research from our industry's most rusted resources... " or "I've been trained and certified by the top experts in our field and I am here to give to you some of what they have recently shared with me..." This is borrowed expertise. You can speak from authority and knowledge even if it is not your authority and knowledge. When I train and certify my team, I remind them to use the information that I gave them AND where they got it from when they "chain-train" it to their teams and so on. If you are a trainer, you must attend every training you can.

You can attend trainings and get certifications to prove your authority on a subject or you can borrow authority. You can say "I have been trained by the industry's best and researched this information from the top authorities," Borrowing authority works well. You can assign much of the authority you borrow. "I work with the top experts in the industry on (insert your topic) subject and they have helped to develop this curriculum and trained me in relaying this to you." Borrowed authority is authority.

Another way to show your capability and to train from a place of knowledge and authority is to have the certifications and training to back the training that you are conducting.

I often refer to myself as a certification junkie. The truth of the matter is I am an education and learning junkie. I love to learn, and all the certifications are a side effect of this wonderful disease. The addiction to lifelong learning is probably why I teach. In teaching, I learn more than I could ever teach. Yes, I said it: teaching is a selfish endeavor for me. When I teach, I get much more than I give. When I am in the front of a class and when I am facilitating the class properly, I learn so much more than I could ever teach. Look at it this way, if I have a room of 25 students and the average experience of each student is 10 years then the collective student experience is 250 years. Compared to my 29 years of experience, I am the weak link in the class. My job is to draw out the unique experiences from each of these students and make their experience, knowledge, and skill part of the collective. During this process, I cannot help but learn. Of course, I develop and follow curriculum that works toward a learning and/or performance goal and share information that I have gathered from classes and experience that I have but I can guarantee that the information transfer goes both ways. This is definitely a win-win situation.

So, the questions are: why do I have so many certifications? Is there value to these certifications? Can there be value in such a broad range of such certifications? To answer these questions, I put together some rules for certifications and education goals for educators and communicators AV/IT:

Begin with the end in mind - (Quote and based on Seven Habits of Highly Effective People – Stephen Covey) – What is the end game? Is there a promotion, target job, target company, target degree or similar goal that a certification or education path will lead you to? Are you looking to develop a specific training program for a sponsor?

Determine the disciplines that you want to follow – Technical, Project Management, Design, etc. – or do you want to head towards multiple disciplines and be a renaissance man (or woman) – this was my goal and why I took so many certifications. My goal was to be multi-disciplined and be as much like Tesla as possible. Tesla is a collaborative communicator, ultimate technology evangelist, and poet. I have set myself on a path to target many disciplines so that I too can be considered a Tesla Teacher.

Tesla Teaching

Set a plan – The concept here is to ask yourself: how do you eat an elephant? The answer is: one bite at a time. Do not try to do it all at once. If someone told me I had to have these certifications, I would have said that it would be impossible, but I took it all in small bites and now I have eaten an elephant.

Use all the resources available to you and barter where you can - you have some skills and knowledge you can trade. Do it. Someone out there needs to know what you know, and they have what you need. Share. I have lived my educational life based on that core belief and that is why I teach and learn to this day. The number one reason that I am by any means successful at what I do (teaching wise) is because I believe in what I do. It is about sharing. Do it!

Take the test or class– so what if you fail? Failing is learning. I will not say if or how many times I have failed certification test…YES, I WILL. I HAVE! And I still have my certifications. Failing can be a study method. If you take and fail a test, then you have seen the test and can better study for the test to take it again and pass.

Enjoy your win – celebrate and brag and help others win too – that is part of sharing.

Keep going – do not lose your certifications. It does not say much when you put on a résumé a lapsed CTS or whatever certification. As a hiring manager, I put very little weight in expired certifications. Keep them renewed. Some of the certifications I have are just to keep other certifications renewed. Sometimes it is a vicious circle, but it is a fun one.

I know I talk a lot about certifications in the section but if you replace the word certification with classes or education or other synonyms for learning, it would all hold true. The certifications I currently have could not have been achieved without learning and that is what it is all about. That is why I believe certifications are all about the BASS. ALL ABOUT THE BASICS that is. EDUCATION and LEARNING is the most basic aspect of certifications and I have never encountered an instance where education and learning is not a good thing.

By the way, I guess I should answer those original questions about why so many certifications.

Q. Why do I have so many certifications?
A. With the goal of lifelong learning, I cannot help but constantly set my own goals for some form of a metrics to make sure that I can prove to myself that I am constantly learning. My certifications are a confirmation to myself that I am constantly learning.

Q. Are there value to these certifications?
A. Absolutely – I have received promotions and new jobs that relate directly to some of my certifications. They also help with credibility with some of the customers I deal with.

Tesla Teaching

Q. Can there be value in such a broad range of such certifications?

A. This was one of my goals. I wanted to target having a very broad range of technical and business certifications. This helps with dealing with customers in business and with helping to relate the technology and the business needs.

In business, in home life and life in general, education is one of the greatest freedoms one can have.

I share information about getting certifications and the education that it takes to get certifications for a couple of reasons. First, it is part of the characteristic of teaching from authority: "Capability." Secondly, I discuss the certification process because it is something you, as a trainer, can relay to your students. Many of your students are lifelong learners and can use this advice as well.

Tesla Teaching

CHAPTER 2

Competence

Provide a Solid, Proven, and Memorable Training

(Your Training Should Work Effectively and Be Remembered by All Who Attend)

Today's scientists have substituted mathematics for experiments, and they wander off through equation after equation, and eventually build a structure which has no relation to reality.
– Nikola Tesla –
Radio Power Will Revolutionize the World (Modern Mechanix & Inventions, July 1934)

Tesla Teaching

Tesla Example – The quote I use to open this chapter is "Today's scientists have substituted mathematics for experiments, and they wander off through equation after equation, and eventually build a structure which has no relation to reality." The reason I use this quote is because it illustrates that Nikola believed in the importance of not only having knowledge, but application of knowledge is important. This was true in his lectures and demonstrations as well.

The Lesson – This book is divided into three parts: knowledge, skill, and attitude. The reason for this, as stated in the preface, is to emphasize the importance of applying knowledge to develop skill and the added blend of caring and having passion to develop attitude. This chapter focuses on the knowledge part and the HOW to conduct training.

This portion of the book is written as if the reader is not a seasoned trainer, presenter, and/or communicator. With this approach, some readers may find the information found in the chapter to be a bit basic. I recommend that the more experienced presenter and communicator glean from this what they can or take some time to take an inventory of their skill set and determine what in this chapter they are doing that makes them the success they are and use it to reinforce their success. Sometimes it can take a reminder like this to make us a better success or more consistent in what they do.

One of the most basic presentation rules that was told to me a very long time ago was one that I believe came from the old IBM training system. Trainers are taught to do three things:
1. Tell them what you are going to tell them.
2. Tell them.
3. Then tell them what you told them.

Tesla Teaching

Down to its lowest level all training can come down to those simple steps. Add in that every story has a beginning, middle and an end and so should every training session.

It is also important to remember that just because you are knowledgeable, experienced, skilled, and have a passion for a subject, does not mean that you are well equipped to teach that subject. As you may have experienced when sitting in some training sessions, just because the trainer knows what he or she is talking about does not mean they can present it well. In this section, we will cover some techniques you can use to become a better communicator. We are assuming you already know the subject matter and that the goal is to work on the presentation and communication skills.

First, let us talk about Target Learning Objectives (TLOs). When developing a training system or training program, it should include TLOs. These are the goals for the training and should be stated up front. TLOs are the answer to the question: "why are we doing this training?"

When developing Target Learning Objectives, it is important to keep some key ideas in mind. The first thing to keep in mind with TLOs is that they need to be specific and measurable. For example, a TLO would finish the following statement: "Upon completion of this course, the participant will..." Since most of us are not running universities or schools of any sort, we can safely assume that the goal of the training is not just the sake of learning. Therefore, the TLO should be connected to a change in behavior, an added skill, and/or an advancement in applicable knowledge that can be measured through testing or some form of certifiable means.

Tesla Teaching

Along with Target Learning Objectives you should focus on a Single-Minded Proposition (SMP). It took me a very long time to learn the lesson that I needed to state the objectives of the training up front. Just like agendas at the beginning of every meeting help to keep the meetings on track, the Target Learning Objective help to keep the training on track. More importantly, these TLOs should feed into a single theme. This Single-Minded Proposition should be stated as such – "If you learn one thing from this training…" When the class knows exactly where the content is heading it helps to connect the dots as they go along.

The SMP allows us to conduct the training with razor-sharp focus. Once you develop your TLOs and SMP and bond them together these should remain in your mind and weave them through your training program or event.

As part of the development of the SMP and the TLOs it is important that you fully understand your audience. In Da Vinci Sales, we used the RIVER technique to identify the characteristics of your sales prospects. Using the acronym, RIVER, you can determine some of the key elements to focus your efforts toward for you to be better in tune with your audience. The RIVER acronym and concept comes from the book *Delivering Knock Your Socks Off Service* from Performance Research Associates. RIVER = Roles, Interests, Values, Expectations, and Requirements. Each of the terms in RIVER is self-explanatory and by using these categories you can make sure that you look at many angles of the person, business, or group of people to help gain more perspective to be more sympathetic.

Using RIVER, one should be able to answer the following questions about your audience:

- Who comprises this group (functions, experience level, degree of involvement, etc.)?
- How much do they already know about the subject (a lot, a little, nothing, etc.)?
- What will be most important to them?
- What "attitudes" might I expect (openness, impatience, hostility, etc.)?
- What's my/our history and experience with them and/or their organization?
- What might be some hurdles (time limits, meeting setting, recent occurrence, etc.)?
- What have participants been told about this session/program?
- What two or three points are the most important ones to get across?

A long time ago, I developed a training system that I use called PEER (Prepare, Evaluate, Execute, Re-Evaluate) training. The PEER has a double meaning. First is the acronym that is shown here: PEER (Prepare, Evaluate, Execute, Re-Evaluate) and secondly is the fact that our peers an important part of our training abilities. That is the second "E" in PEER – EVALUATE. This is not the evaluation that attendees do after the execution of the event. The evaluation that PEER refers to is the one that should be done BEFORE the execution of the event and should be done by one of our peers.

Having a peer observe your training and communication skills, using a predetermined set of criteria, is very valuable. These peers are best suited to assist in the development of your training skills and training/communications programs. This is key.

Tesla Teaching

We are our worst critics and we cannot objectively evaluate our own skills as trainers/presenters/communicators. One of the most valuable tools you can avail yourself to is to have one of your peers objectively evaluate your presentation and communication skills.

In the figure below you will see an example of an evaluation that can be used by one of your peers to evaluate your presentation and communication skills:

PREPARATION - SMILE	Y	N	NOTES
Students – I know who my audience is – I ask questions to find out.	☐	☐	
Materials – I give out supporting documents and support take-aways.	☐	☐	
Instructor – I am the appropriate person to cover the material.	☐	☐	
Listen – I do more listening and asking questions. It's about students.	☐	☐	
Environment – My audience is comfortable. I take command.	☐	☐	
GENERAL APPEARANCE	Y	N	
Dress is crisp and is one step above the audience.	☐	☐	
Posture is straight and relaxed.	☐	☐	
Distracting movement minimal, natural (rocking, hands in pockets, etc.).	☐	☐	
If I smoke/around smokers I have prepared properly, breath and clothing.	☐	☐	
Smile and seem approachable.	☐	☐	
VOCAL QUALITY AND TECHNIQUE	Y	N	
Voice is easy to hear without being too loud.	☐	☐	
Words are clearly articulated.	☐	☐	
Pacing is good – neither too slow nor too fast.	☐	☐	
Vocal tone is pleasant – neither grating nor nasal.	☐	☐	
Energy level shows interest and enthusiasm.	☐	☐	
I lean forward when I talk,	☐	☐	
I whisper to make a point.	☐	☐	
I stand to present.	☐	☐	
I am animated.	☐	☐	
I avoid fidgeting (including with hands in pocket).	☐	☐	
PRESENTATION TECHNIQUES	Y	N	
Proper use of gestures – too little seems dull, too much is distracting.	☐	☐	
Body language – does it match message.	☐	☐	
Eye contact –appropriate amount of eye contact (3 sec).	☐	☐	
Eyes are clear and bright.	☐	☐	
Passion and emotion is evident in speaking and demonstration.	☐	☐	
Message is complete and accurate.	☐	☐	
I use a story to engage.	☐	☐	
I get laughs an appropriate amount of time.	☐	☐	
My presentation has a common theme.	☐	☐	
Cover what you're going to tell, tell, and what you told them.	☐	☐	
There is a post event action.	☐	☐	

General presentation posture (circle one or more).

Notes:

Tesla Teaching

Figure 10

In Chapter 1, I mentioned that well over 90% of the training programs out there (based on my own observations) are developed using the presentation (PowerPoint). Think about how wrong this is. The goal is not the presentation. The goal is so much more. So, I will say it now if I did not say it clear enough before: DO NOT USE POWERPOINT to develop your training! PowerPoint is only one of the tools used to deliver part of the training or materials that supports a message in communication.

There are many more tools required for your training program. Another one of the tools is a lesson plan. The lesson plan works towards goals that have been established and the gaps that have been identified. Here are some of the major elements of the lesson plan:

Professional trainers create and follow a lesson plan for most programs. These are reusable documents that do several things for you. A lesson plan will show you an overview summary of the whole program using key words. As you are going through the event the lesson plan will remind you of what comes next. Just before the training, if you want to make an on the spot adjustment, the lesson plan will give you a way to skip whole sections of the program and in the same spirit, help you keep a record of parts not done for any given group. The lesson plan contains the timeline for the event and a complete breakdown by subject so you can use it to distribute to all the participants so they can keep track of the timeline with you. Once the event is over, you can compare the actual event time to planned time so you can adjust the next time. It is very important to keep track, and factor in, break times and adjust for future deliveries of the event. This is the one item that is the hardest to predict and feedback from actual events is very valuable.

Tesla Teaching

Below is an example of an over simplified lesson plan for a Tesla Teaching class:

Tesla Teaching

Program date/location: _____

Subject/ Ideas	Time: Plan/Actual
Welcome, Orientation, and Overview Greet and welcome group. Introduce yourself and other leaders. Have group introduce themselves if they haven't met. Give upbeat kickoff. Invite participation. Two promises: Challenge & act. Review target objectives. Explain dual role: medium is the message.	10 Minutes
What makes training good Ask group what they think. Pad responses. Summarize from slide: Clearly-stated objectives. Understand audience. Appropriate/application based content. Good tools. Effective delivery. Participant engagement.	15 Minutes
Target Learning Objectives Explain this is a Tesla term. What makes them valid: Clearly stated up front. Describe outcomes. Specific. Performance-based. Address attitude, knowledge, or skill. Will vary by group. Teach to these.	10 Minutes

Figure 11

This lesson plan does not have nearly enough detail in it, but it gets the point across. The lesson plan is something you do long before you open PowerPoint.

Tesla Teaching

Above is a very basic lesson plan. I cannot stress enough that this lesson plan is not one that I would use for teaching but a fair enough one to illustrate the concept. I will later give better examples of the actual lesson plan. I will also state that the openings I use are quite different. By this, I mean I use different icebreakers or exercises to get the class going. It is important to be different in your openings and introductions these days.

What matters here is that everything is planned to the minute and every detail is planned. Once the bulk of the planning is done (section by section), the next step could be that the lesson be planned (content wise).

Below is an example of how the content could be planned in detail. Again, the content is not necessarily planned in PowerPoint. It is more important that the message and supporting multimedia is considered. If the technology fails, the media can be transferred to whatever medium is available (i.e. whiteboard, overhead projector, paper, and pencil, etc.). The trainer and the content are what matters most in how the information is transferred to the listener and more importantly, to create an engaged listener (participant).

This connection from content and trainer to listener is where cleverness enters the equation.

Tesla Teaching

CHAPTER 3

Cleverness

Teach in New Ways to Match Learner's Requirements

(Add New Methods and Technology to Meet the Expectations of New Learners. Meet the Needs of Attendees Who Recently Came Out of Advanced Learning Environments – Collaboration is Key)

"The day science begins to study non-physical phenomena; it will make more progress in one decade than in all the previous centuries of its existence."
> – Nikola Tesla –
> Unknown source

Tesla Teaching

Tesla Example – Tesla became known as a magician in some instances. This was because how he gave his presentations to the public on AC versus DC electricity. He would hold a light bulb in one of his hands and allow his Tesla Coil nearby to light it. This was an incredible presentation on how AC worked and how wireless power could one day be achieved. The everyday person would not have been able to fathom a technical presentation from Tesla. but Tesla's ability to be the technical communicator allowed him to CLEVERLY connect with his audience in a way the audience could hear the content and engage. In Tesla's demonstrations, each piece of equipment was new, of his own design, and fabricated in his own workshop. The same demonstration was seldom repeated from one appearance to the next.

The Lesson – The lesson here is that no matter how knowledgeable and skilled we are and no matter how much experience and attitude we have, we still need to cleverly engage our audiences. Tesla teaches us by example that even with his extreme attitude, skill, and knowledge; he still needed to use additional techniques to have his message translate to his audience. To truly connect and have his learners own the message, he deployed some utterly innovative and CLEVER methods of showmanship and storytelling. Many attendees believed much of what he was saying was storytelling because it seemed so farfetched. The beauty of it was that it was coming from a man who was out of his own time and speaking of future stories. For example, Tesla had to wait 16 years to see his fated vision of harnessing the power of Niagara Falls.

Tesla Teaching

In the preface (p. 23, figure 5), I discuss the need for balancing technology, place, and people. The added importance is that you must use the available technology in the optimal environment (place) in a way that you can best add your CLEVER spin and unique flare.

I make this sound easy, but I do want to share that I understand that it is a lot easier said than done. There is some good news here though. I want you to think about this. You may have to reread this section a couple of times because I will have a hard time phrasing it properly. Think about some of the training sessions you have been through. When you sat down, did you think to yourself: "I hope this presenter sucks?" Have you ever gone to a training session and known that the material was going to be relevant and that the location and training space were optimal for the training? Was the technology perfect for this training and then you knew that the trainer was wrong, and you thought it would be great anyway? I do not think this ever happens this way. So why do I bring this up at this section in the book? Well I want to emphasize that almost every participant, in every training, is hoping that the trainer is going to be great. Your audience is on your side. This is a great position to be in and should be quite encouraging.

With that encouraging news, you should feel empowered to be yourself and not feel that as a trainer you need to emulate anyone else. When I mentor trainers, this is one of the pitfalls fall into. Here is what I have observed. I tend to tell a lot of jokes when I conduct training. I do this because it is part of my natural personality and it helps me to connect my students to the material. The jokes are usually topical and relate to the content in some way. When I am teaching another trainer, they take my materials and resources and most often try to train the material in the same way I do, jokes and all. Eventually, they learn that they need to make it their own and use their own style, but it is a tough lesson. This lesson is often learned after they feel the pain of rough reviews and awkward missed connections in classes.

The important message is that in order for you to add the "You Factor" and truly make the message yours, and to add a way to CLEVERLY connect the message to the audience, you need to make it yours and not emulate someone else's way of training. I want to bring it back around and emphasize that this is a completely safe environment to be yourself because here the audience is on your side and absolutely wants you to succeed. Be yourself and add your "You Factor," whatever that "You Factor" is.

It may take time for you to achieve a level of comfort in adding a "You Factor". When you are this comfortable, you will connect and it will add a level of being able to think on your feet and act swiftly in training that will make you the CLEVER trainer that Nikola was.

Your "You Factor" is what will add the level of CLEVERNESS that makes the connection that will drive the content for your learners.

One example of my "You Factor" is I incorporate juggling and riding a unicycle while I teach an AV/IT class. This is a class on IT fundamentals for AV professionals. I use juggling to help make an important connection during my training, to get people on their feet, keep people engaged and active, and to transition to and from breaks. During my three-day course, I teach the participants how to juggle and (more importantly) I train IT for AV people. These are people who know audio and video technology well. Here is how I use the juggling as a tie into the course:
- Students pair up (there is a lesson tied in later about mitigating risks using partnering and shared risk techniques).

Tesla Teaching

- The three juggling balls are used to represent the major categories of disciplines in the industry (Audio, Video, and IT).
- Each student identifies which discipline they are strongest in and during the first juggling exercise they toss that juggling ball from their dominant hand to their partner back and forth from hand to hand.
  - Their partner's job is to retrieve bad throws and not allow the thrower to move at all. (The lesson here is that if a bad throw is made the student's partner is the one who pays the price. We found that the thrower makes a lot of more accurate throws when they are impacting someone else)
- In the second juggling exercise, the student chooses their second strongest discipline and now the students stand face to face with their partner. The exercise is throw-throw and their partner are catch-catch. Again, we see that the focus is much stronger on accurate throws when the other person is subject to chasing down errant throws. The side effect of the exercise is that the partners learn a rhythm of throw-throw, catch-catch that ultimately is all there is to juggling.
- Now the juggler takes on the third task and their partner's job are to just receive three throws. So, the rhythm becomes, throw-throw-throw. As the receiver you realize that you must clear one of your hands to receive the third ball. The instinct becomes throw-throw-throw catch-catch, throw-throw, catch-catch, and so on.

All of these lessons tie in together to point out that juggling becomes easier when you have a partner to chase your dropped juggles (if you are learning IT and you have a partner that knows IT, you can work together to pick up the missed opportunities). Any task that looks too complicated can be broken down into steps and be taught or learned or managed by partnering and mitigating risks.

Ultimately the lessons went much deeper in IT but it made for memorable experiences and we had fun during these trainings by using some of my "You Factor" and I add my CLEVERNESS to engage students and make the content memorable for them. To this day, I still have students come up to me who comment on how the class, content, and even the juggling changed the way they approach certain professional development subjects. I am not the end all in any manner of speaking. I am fortunate to have chanced upon a couple of neat ways of engaging audiences that leverage my "You Factor." The challenge is always there; can you find yours and use it?

Another way I would like to illustrate this is to use the word engagement. In my trainings, I use a lot of mnemonics. In this example, the word engagement is one of my mnemonics. I present the three E's of EngagEmEnt.

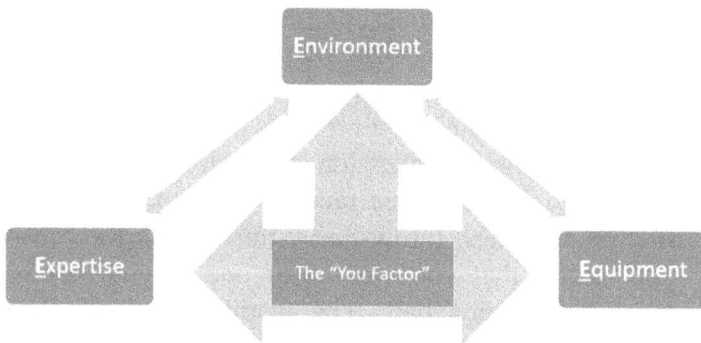

Figure 12

The three E's of EngagEmEnt show that when the environment is right, the right equipment is used and when the presenter has the right knowledge, skill, and experience, the equation is not complete. EngagEmEnt requires the uniqueness of the "You Factor" from the trainer. Another example from Tesla is when he presented the "Egg of Columbus."

Tesla Teaching

Here is the story of the "Egg of Columbus" and how Tesla uses his CLEVERNESS to train. Tesla's version of the "Egg of Columbus" in (with maybe some paraphrasing) his own words:

In hopes of getting financial support, Dr. Tesla had approached a prominent lawyer and Wall Street capitalist and his friend, a well-known engineer who was also head of one of the big corporations in New York The engineer was a practical expert who knew of the failures in the industrial exploitation of alternating current and was distinctly prejudiced to a point of not caring even to witness some tests. After several discouraging meetings, Dr. Tesla had an inspiration (one that led to his CLEVER presentation/training method.) Everybody has heard of the "Egg of Columbus." The saying goes that at a certain dinner the great explorer Columbus asked some scoffers of his project to balance an egg on its end. They tried it in vain. He then took it and cracking the shell slightly by a gentle blow, made it stand upright. This may be a myth, but the fact is that he was granted an audience by Isabella, the Queen of Spain, and won her support. He said to these men, "Do you know the story of the Egg of Columbus?" They did. "Well," he continued, "what if I could make an egg stand on the pointed end without cracking the shell?" "If you could do this, we would admit that you had done Columbus one better." "And would you be willing to go out of your way as much as Queen Isabella?" "We have no crown jewels to pawn," said the lawyer, who was a wit, "but there are a few ducats in our buckskins, and we might help you to an extent."

Tesla was able to achieve this feat using electromagnetic principles with AC, not only convincing his investors by delivering on his promise but also by adding his own 'spin' to the solution.

Tesla Teaching

In the previous example, Tesla was able to teach using a story telling method and bring a very complex and controversial (Chapter 7) topic and use his <u>E</u>ngag<u>E</u>m<u>E</u>nt abilities to relay his message.

As I mentioned, I use a lot of mnemonics in my training. That is part of my "You Factor." I also mentioned that I tell a lot of jokes. I should also mention that CLEVERNESS could also include something that makes the training memorable. In the case of training that I have come up with for the collaboration and presentation solutions at WolfVision, I have tried to add combination of some silliness and mnemonics to the training for my spin on CLEVERNESS.

> The training includes the importance of the watchwords for AV/IT: Flexibility, Reliability, Affordability, and Scalability. When I looked at these watchwords, I wanted to make sure they became memorable to the class. My mind kicked in to 12-year-old mode. I decided that farts are memorable and silly. Who could forget it if I included farts in my training? So, since WolfVision is trusted globally by some of the largest corporations in our industry add the "T" from trusted and you have all you need for the acronym/mnemonic: "FARTS." This may not be your style and it did not land me a job in marketing at WolfVision, but it can hopefully illustrate that your CLEVERNESS can make a class memorable. It is this that makes the difference from your skill, knowledge, and experience. How you relay the skill, knowledge, and experience through CLEVERNESS is what really matters.

Tesla Teaching

Now that the class has memorized the watchwords, I needed them to understand the features of the product. The product, Cynap is a media-management solution for collaboration, presentation, and conferencing. The actual features include presentation of wired and wireless content (AV/IT), conferencing collaboration through annotation/whiteboarding, PC replacement content player–Office 365, presentation system, and simultaneous streaming and recording.

For these students to remember all these features and to make a tie into the watchwords, I made the acronym/mnemonic: "CRAMPS."

CRAMPS
C = Collaboration / Conferencing (WebRTC/Skype4Biz)
R = Recording / Streaming (Simultaneous)
A = Annotation and Whiteboarding
M = Media Player (PC Replacement/Office 365)
P = Presentation/BYOD Viewer (Multiview 4 windows)
S = System (all-in-one)

CRAMPS and FARTS will never make it into marketing documents, but the attendees of the face-to-face training will never forget the watchwords or the specifications of the Cynap product.

Tesla Teaching

Below you will find some methods by category on ways to CLEVERLY train. Many of these CLEVER teaching methods are often used in combination and it is and art and science on how to balance the use of these and when to do so:

- Facilitation
- Dynamic Content Creation
- Role Play
- Contests and Rewards
- Quizzing and Practice
- Listening
- Brainstorming
- Using Internal and External Resources
- Use and Encourage Humor
- Visual Aids, Props, Products and Other Hardware

Tesla Teaching

Here is a little more information on each of these:

Facilitation – When conducting a training session where many peers and other industry professionals are the students, facilitation is a good method to use. Facilitation has the participants engage a lot more than the typical presentations. Because the participants usually have much of the content spread amongst the group, your job can often be to just guide the participants to a consensus in the steps to get to the same result and to navigate the discussions to stay on the Target Learning Objectives. Your ability to facilitate is still dependent on your knowledge, skill, and attitude, but how you add your "You Factor" so that you manage the discussions, keep the group engaged and have everyone arrive at the same result remains a key value-add. The way I try to do this is by breaking the class into small groups and assign subjects to these groups. Each group will work through a portion of the TLOs and present their findings. The role I play is to guide them and provide insights, questions and even glean additional information that the group knew but did not know they knew.

Collaboration – Using the above technique, facilitation allows a teacher to also use collaboration. Most adult learners have the need to contribute to the learning process. Some adult learners need to contribute to the content, while others need to contribute through discussion and share their experience. We also have some adult learners that are very good at demonstrating skills but are not good at carrying on discussions. When a teacher can facilitate well and can engage the collaboration process, learning can quite be fruitful for many.

Dynamic Content Creation – Whether you use flipcharts, a Visualizer (document camera), an annotator over live content, or some other means of creating content on the fly, you have a way to reach your audience in a meaningful way.

Role Play– A great example of when this comes in handy is during sales training. Having some of the students act as the customer and others act as the sale person and then going through an exercise of sales or needs analysis can be very useful and can drive home some very important lessons. This is true for many other scenarios. This technique works very well when you need the students to rehearse a behavior and/or learn from making a mistake in a safe environment.

Contests and Rewards – This is a good time to get people to work on something that may require a skill to be performed as well as something that is time sensitive. This can also help when you need to evaluate whether someone needs to perform a skill that needs to be measured. You can also have the students measure each other. Competitions can be fun and can reinforce learning in a memorable way.

Quizzing and Practice – Repetition is very important. Using quizzing can be very helpful to this end and this can reinforce skills as well. Practice makes perfect.

Listening – Having the student do teach-backs and allowing you to act as the student is a great technique to have the students "own" the content, give you a break when the class sizes are large, and shows you are engaged by your active listening.

Brainstorming – Facilitating a brainstorming session is a great way to engage learners. One method to do this is to brainstorm on possible questions that could be developed from the content that was presented. As you collect possible questions you have the brainstorm on possible questions and study methods. They are developing the content for the course as you go. Based on your skill, experience, and knowledge you guide and facilitate the brainstorming session.

Using Internal and External Resources – Here I am recommending that you use the resources that are in the room. Because this book is mostly addressing the adult learning market, you are likely to find that many of your attendees are Subject Matter Experts in many of the areas that you are teaching in. You can borrow some of their expertise and guide the discussions using the techniques above to collaborate and coordinate the thoughts and brainstorming. When the resources are not in the class, you can invite them in for guest speaking sessions. Your students will never be offended or bothered with the fact that you have to bring in guests to speak in your classes. I later refer to this as "borrowing authority" and your student will still assign that authority to you when you are the one who will bolster them to learn what they need to know,

Use and Encourage Humor – One of the biggest barriers to learning is stress. There is a tough balance between having enough stress to drive the learner to keeping a level of importance and knowing the need for learning the topic/subject. On the flipside, there is also the need to relieve stress in the classroom environment and one of the best ways to do this is through humor. This is where another tough balance comes in; where if you are not naturally funny you should not try to force yourself to be. Therefore, this section is titled Use and Encourage Humor. If you are not naturally the joke teller or naturally funny, then there are other ways to encourage humor in class. It is important to be yourself above all other things. In the Bonus Chapter, there is an entire section on being funny and using humor.

Visual Aids, Props, Products, and Other Hardware – Many learners need hands-on and tactile re-enforcement. It is important to remember that visual aids, props, products, and such should be used to re-enforce content. I can almost guarantee that when you use hardware of any sort as the content instead of in support of the content, it will fail. Visual aids should support and should not repeat the content. Stay away from PowerPoint with long paragraphs, use visuals and pictures. Hardware should be supportive, but knowledge and skill still trump all.

CHAPTER 4

Curiosity

Be Like Your Learners, Always Ask Why
Why? Why? Why?

(Anticipate the Questions That You Will Hear and Know
How You Will Answer – Rehearsal Is Key)

*"Life is and will ever remain an equation
incapable of solution, but it contains certain known
factors."*
– Nikola Tesla –
A Machine to End War, Liberty, February 1937

Tesla Teaching

Tesla Example – When Tesla was a young man, he was curious about many things. One of those things was powered flight. He was so curious he wanted to study it in ways that school and lessons could not fulfill this curiosity. Once he even took a spinning disc and glued June Bugs to it to act motors. It took 16 June Bugs to power his spinning disk.

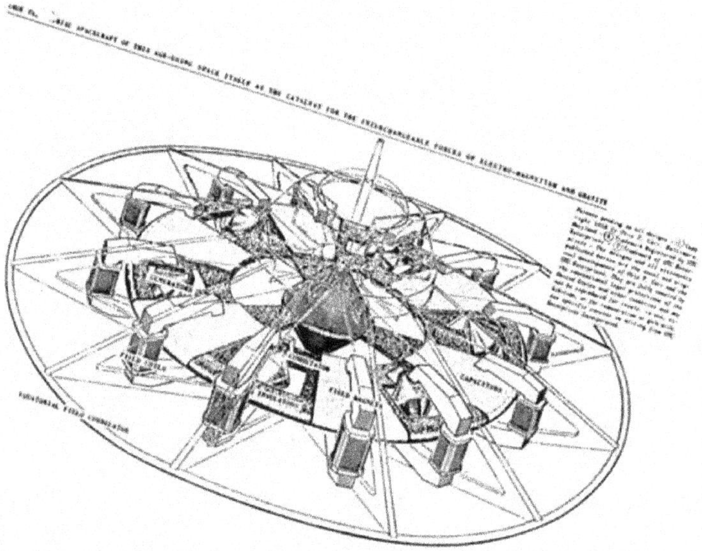

Figure 13

Tesla's curiosity was constant throughout his life. He often watched pigeons in flight around his home and this too piqued his curiosity. As part of his study and to quell his curiosity, he attempted the classic umbrella flight maneuver. Even though this attempt at flight from the top of a barn resulted in many days recovering in bed, this event did not stop his curiosity.

The Lesson – Here we can learn that even one of the most intelligent people on the planet can remain curious. Lifelong learning was one of Nikola's most valuable traits. We also learn that with Nikola's curiosity, he was not afraid to fail.

Tesla Teaching

Even toward the end of his life, he took chances with wireless power, the death ray, and other risky endeavors. He took the risk to learn new things and because of that, he was able to be a better teacher.

Curiosity does not always mean that we are successful. We must be willing to fail to learn. This same statement holds true when we want to teach. We must be willing to fail if we want to teach. We must be willing to fail before we can succeed as teachers or we can never stretch and reach new levels of connection with our students. When Nikola was young, he was not afraid to fail. He wanted to learn how clocks worked so he would often take them apart. "At this I was always successful," Nikola said. Then he would try to rebuild them. "At this, I often failed." These statements come from the same person who could have been the person who made THE most important discoveries and impacts in science in our age. How amazing is that he can admit his failures and what it took for him to learn how to learn.

Tesla Teaching

Satisfying Curiosity by Creating "So What?" Training

Among many attributes, it takes humility, an inquisitive nature, and great listening skills to be a good trainer. Those attributes seem almost obvious, right? Okay, I will give you that. I think what takes a little more thought and may not be as obvious is the inquisitive nature that is required to be a great trainer. This inquisitive nature requires more than just a curiosity about how things work, how people interact and how to creatively solve problems. You also need to constantly wonder what other people are wondering, especially what your students are wondering. Therefore, I titled this part of the chapter "So What?" Training. You need to be constantly asking yourself "So What?" in the same way your students would be. You should be doing this as if your students are asking the question as you make every point you are making or concept you are covering. You should be hearing your student's voice saying, "So What?" You need to be covering the "what is in it for me factor."

Your classes, lunch and learns and even your sales meetings with your students/customers, will be at least 10X more productive if you spend time before the meeting rehearsing what your approach is going to be based on the research you have done on the customer's pains, buying process, and technology expertise. You can then focus your rehearsal around knowing the answers to their "So What's?" The students/customer will thank you for not wasting their time. Notice that I assume you research the pains, buying process and technical expertise for the customers/students (buyers) **prior** to your meeting. I also assume you are meeting with students/customers/buyers (decision makers) and that you rehearse your meeting. I have done countless sales presentations and training and I still rehearse almost every time to some degree. If I ever get to the point where I stop rehearsing and stop caring enough to do so, it will be time to hang it up.

Using the "So What?" method allows you to get to the three core questions sooner in the training / sales meeting / conversation. For this, you should have answers to these three core questions prepared before the training/meeting ever starts:

1. Why do something? Have you given the customer a compelling reason for learning/action? Have you made the customer realize a pain or competitive disadvantage he/she was not aware of? This is sometimes a tough one to remember because when you are passionate about your products or solutions. They seem like a no brainer solution and you may forget that you need to make a compelling presentation or "argument" for it to your customers. Not everyone sees the obviousness of the value of the solutions you provide as you do. You need to pretend that the customer knows nothing of our business and that they are always saying "So What?" This just happened to me when I was telling people about grAVITation TECH. To me, it was so obvious that our industry needed training and that I did not need a clear value statement, but my customer needed to hear it from me. I cannot tell you how many lessons I have learned from my customers. For training, did your TLO provide a compelling reason for the student to learn this topic? Is the "why I need to learn this" important to them?

This brings up a minor point I would like to share while it is on my mind. I want to share with you that customers/students are, often, willing to help you succeed. I say this because in the above example and in many examples, the customer has been willing to teach me when I needed it. When you are willing to listen, the customer/student will guide you toward how to communicate better with them. Just remember to constantly look for their clues. In the case of when I was talking about grAVITation TECH, the customer was willing to share that I did not start at the right level, but I was open enough to allow them to share that. Had I been communicating in a manner that had them thinking that their statement would have sounded or been taken as an insult, they would have left it alone. Be open to correction and guidance from your audience.

2. Why do something now? Have you convinced your customer of the urgency of the situation (have you given them a good reason to learn this topic now?)? Have you even tried to? Or did you just go with the customer's budget and timing? One of the keys to" So What?" training is to assign urgency for the customer. You need to guide the customer in setting the expectations and understanding of the timeline. They need to understand the detrimental impact of waiting to implement your training. By showing the customer the cost of not getting their training in now or delaying action, you assign urgency to the implementation of your training. Whether it is a continued lack or lessened productivity or loss of customers because of perceived lack of innovation (example being not invested in collaborative solutions), these examples need to be shown in strategic, political (competitive landscape), financial or cultural terms. These are the areas that people of power (decision makers) are focused. There are many ROI, TCO, ROO and other top end calculators (free from vendors in our industry)

out there to use for this purpose. These are typical in selling to C-Level people, but they are helpful in making the business case and showing your strategic literacy when working with all types of key decision makers.

3. Why do it with you? Have you made the compelling case for the customer to select you as a training source? People do business with people they like but that is after all the other things are said and done. And by the way, no training company or salesperson has a relationship quota. It is great if you make a lot of friends out there, but you need business partners more. So, have you given the students/customer the compelling reasons to learn from you? These reasons have more to do with your knowledge, skill, and attitude and your "You Factor,"

The whole idea is to answer the "So What's?" before they are ever asked.

Just imagine that there is a little version of your students sitting on your shoulder. That little version of your student is there while you are rehearsing in the mirror the night before or while you are driving on your way to the big training. He/she is there saying: "SO WHAT, SO WHAT, SO WHAT?!?!?!" If you remember that, you are half way to a successful training session. Remember the preparation determines half the outcome. Keep listening to that "SO WHAT, SO WHAT, SO WHAT?!?!?!" Have your answers ready and you'll knock them dead!

Tesla Teaching

CHAPTER 5

Commitment

Acting In Accordance With Your Purpose Even In The
Face Of Extreme Opposition

(Having Insight as to Your Own Beliefs and Alignment)

The desire that guides me in all I do is the desire to harness the forces of nature to the service of mankind."
– Nikola Tesla –
Radio Power Will Revolutionize the World (Modern Mechanix & Inventions, July, 1934)

Tesla Teaching

Tesla Example – In this section, I tend to think of the term commitment and conviction almost synonymously. Tesla showed his conviction a few times in a strong way. The first illustration I can think of is when he declined the royalties to be paid to him from the horsepower from Niagara Falls and the use of his improved dynamos. Tesla declined payment from Westinghouse of $2 per horsepower to avoid Westinghouse from going bankrupt. This was completely based on his commitment to his friend and partner, Westinghouse.

Another case of Tesla living the example of commitment was when Tesla walked away from Edison. Edison had cheated Tesla out of a $50K bonus. Although the dispute was considerable, Edison was willing to give Tesla a raise of over 50% to try to resolve the conflict but because Tesla thought it was so important to live up to his commitments, he walked away instead.

One last example I would give of how Tesla lived such an example of commitment and conviction was when he was searching for investors and finally found them. Initially, he turned them down because they wanted him to start immediately. He turned them down because he was digging ditches at the time and he was not finished. He was committed to finishing and insisted on sticking to that commitment before he started on their project. He also initially turned down these investors because they didn't believe in his inventions and theories and they were hedging their bets by investing in other competing theories. He confronted them and forced them to invest in just his ideas or not at all. They chose him.

Tesla Teaching

The Lesson – What was the result of Tesla living up to his convictions? Thank goodness that we are using a historical figure to measure this because we don't always see the results of this in the short term. With Tesla, we can see that, over time, he lived according to his convictions and he ultimately was rewarded. By turning down the offers to settle and make compromises, Nikola found investors that believed in him, his inventions, and ultimately invested. These investments allowed Tesla to start his own company of his own name.

Part of getting students to engage is having them take ownership of the content. What better way can you get for them to take ownership of the content than to feel convicted. Passion and purpose are important to the learning process. If you, as an instructor / teacher, are not convicted then how can you expect your students to be? I said it earlier but the day I stop caring about what I am teaching, is the day I need to stop.

So how do we relay what we are teaching is meaningful to use and is part of our belief system? There are three major points that need to be made to relay that the training is part of commitment / conviction:

1. Tell a personal story connecting the content to yourself, your family, or your career.
2. Tie information in on how the same content has improved the way you do business or how not having it caused you hardship.
3. Share as many "aha" moments that tie into the key target learning objectives that naturally fit within the conversation of the training.

The three points that we are referring to is how this content has impacted your life in your knowledge, skill and attitude. In this respect, you should share personal insights where appropriate. It is okay to be human while you are a trainer and the emotional connection you make between yourself, your content, and your students does matter.

This second part of this section is focused on ways to get the instructor and student behind the training. Whether you are supporting an entire training program or a single event, the success is largely dependent on buy in. The more buy in you get from trainers, students and sponsors, the more likely the training will be a success.

At WolfVision, Inc. USA we recently went through an exercise where we looked at our Vision, Mission, and Principles. In order to plan a strategy and execute a tactical plan it is important to have a unified vision, mission. and a clear set of principles that the team can operate from. This is no different when setting up training for a company or individual training sessions. This is important because this helps lay a foundation for why the training is taking place and why each trainer and student needs to get behind the training.

If we take a look at the example of the WolfVision, Inc. USA Vision, Mission, and Principles it may help. First, it is important to why the structure of why the Vision, Mission, and Principles is used.

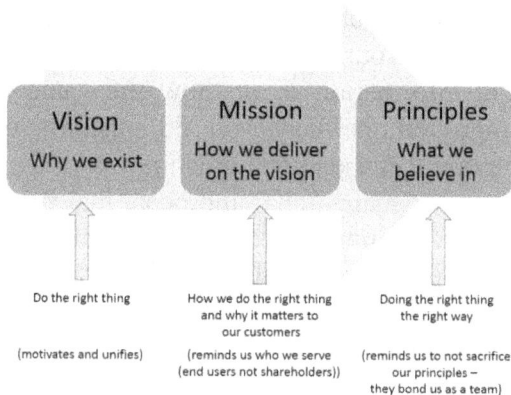

Vision	Mission	Principles
Why we exist	How we deliver on the vision	What we believe in
Do the right thing	How we do the right thing and why it matters to our customers	Doing the right thing the right way
(motivates and unifies)	(reminds us who we serve (end users not shareholders))	(reminds us to not sacrifice our principles – they bond us as a team)

Figure 14

Tesla Teaching

Using the Vision / Mission / Principle method helps us to follow a train of thought that if we all can get behind one clear, concise, consistent message, then we can all head in the same direction more efficiently. Shouldn't training work the same way? So how do we make training follow this type of format and turn that into a way of getting commitment and conviction in your training. Firstly, we should probably understand what the definitions of the Vision / Mission and Principles are:

Vision: Is thought of as the "Why Are We Here?" statement. This is used to make the class create a vision of a unified direction of what is our end goal and how the class would like to be seen from an outsider's perspective. It helps to define what we do. Defining this is easy for courses like lifesavers and first responders because the vision is very apparent. Other classes that don't have such an easily apparent vision have to look further down the road to remember why they are there. The key point is to look at the end goal and focus on the purpose and passion. For example, I teach CTS study groups. The Vision is not to get people to pass their CTS exam but possibly to help people improve their career paths and to make lives better through professional development.

Mission: Once we know the Vision, the Mission becomes a little clearer. The Mission is how we deliver on the Vision. This also helps to define why what we do matters. In the case of the example I used, where I teach CTS study groups, I would say that the Mission is:: to grow as many sales, sales support people and project professionals as possible while maintaining highest quality training with the highest integrity on the market.

Principles: This is a definition of how we do what we do by doing it right. Another way of saying this is how we behave. In the case of the CTS training I provide, we could add that we train with integrity and in an environment that is

73

conducive to learning where all students feel welcome and comfortable.

The example of an actual VISION / MISSION / PRINCIPLES statement that I put into action was with WolfVision. The important thing to remember here was that this was not just something to put on the wall. This was something we used to ingest and get behind, so that when people asked why we do what we do, or what we believe in, we had our answer and we believed it. I have shared this statement below:

Vision: To be known as a key provider of equipment, solutions, support, and services that make our world better through simplifying and improving communications.

Mission: Provide high quality, innovative communication and collaboration systems with support and services that all significantly contribute to our user's ability to cure diseases, inspire learning and creativity, build wealth, ensure justice, keep the peace, solve problems, and increase joy through simplifying and improving communication.

Principles: As a company, we believe our employees are our most valuable resource and we invest in their personal and professional development. We rely on their contribution to our common goal of creativities innovation in an environment that encourages open, honest, tolerant and respectful treatment of our employees and partners. We all seek a relationship of transparency, respect, trust, cooperation and mutual learning at all levels (internally and externally). Our operating principles also include that we always strive for long-term success and long-term collaborative relationships with our partners and vendors. We choose to deliver quality and durability over price. We will seek value for our partners whenever possible. We desire to remain financially responsible/independent and forward-looking. As a forward-looking company, we drive ourselves to remain respectfully competitive and market driven. We are constantly capturing the voice of the customer and develop solutions with their needs in mind. Because our

Tesla Teaching

TEAM supports a worldwide company, we will always stay true to the core values of modern society, and recognize the applicable laws of each respective country and its institutions. We will consciously work to conserve natural resources, and pass on an intact world to future generations. We know what we do and how we sell matters and we will behave as such.

Commitment to process and consistency:

One of the other commitments you should make to your training or your training program is to the process and to consistency. One way to deliver on this commitment is to approach your training with a project management perspective. Project managers live by the "Iron Triangle". The "Iron Triangle" is a project management law that states that the three sides of the triangle are made up of time, scope, and cost. Since the sides are made of iron, if one side changes so must the others. This illustrates that when managing a project, such as training, if time, scope, or cost changes so must one of the others.

For example: if you are working on a training project for a customer and they need to add a section or topic to the training then the cost would go up and so would the time. This illustrates that when the scope changed so did the time and cost. When you try to break this law, then you sacrifice quality or you increase risk.

The illustration below shows how the Iron Triangle locks risk and quality in to the sides of time, scope, and cost:

Figure 15

Your commitment is to manage your training programs and projects with the same discipline that project managers do with formalize project management systems.

Commitment to quality:

Another important consideration about commitment and training is making a commitment to quality in training. When you do training for AIA (the American Institute of Architects) they have you sign a quality statement regarding your training. This is your commitment to them that your training will meet a certain level of quality every time you present for them. I know many organizations ask trainers to provide this type of commitment.

It is a good practice to have this as part of every training engagement that you take on. This will be a reminder of the bar you have set for your trainings. You could include something, like the following, at the beginning of every training engagement:

Another commitment that you should make is related to the previous one. This one builds on the quality that falls within the Iron Triangle, but should stand on its own. Quality should have its own focus. I studied LEAN Six Sigma quality management / process improvement. Many people believe Six Sigma process improvement only applies to manufacturing lines and ways of improving to make a particular product. But if you look at the fact that as a trainer, your product is your training, then Six Sigma process improvement can be applied to improving your product line and helps for you to deliver quality nearly all of the time.

Six Sigma training systems: Six Sigma and Sales Process Improvement

Organizational issues can be found by using the Six Sigma DMAIC methods for continuous improvement. I will go into a bit more detail about the DMAIC methods and give an overview of Six Sigma. DMAIC stands for Define, Measure, Analyze, Improve and Control. I will talk about how Six Sigma and the DMAIC method fit into training and I will go into detail about the DMAIC method.

If you have never heard of Six Sigma that probably makes this a bit easier to read but if you have heard of it, I will need you to let go of any possible preconceptions you may have and give what I am saying a chance. The reason I say it may be easier to accept Six Sigma if you've never heard of it is because five to ten years back, Six Sigma was being used by a lot of organizations to justify a process re-engineering effort that was often crafted by executive management and boards to appease shareholders. It was often implemented incorrectly and used as "house cleaning" projects to justify layoffs. There was a lot of promoting of Six Sigma in the manufacturing world and it started to be known solely for manufacturing defect improvement. The two biggest misconceptions about Six Sigma and the DMAIC method are that it is just for manufacturing and that it is a way to reduce your staffing requirements. As you read on, I will try to show you that Six Sigma is much more than a manufacturing line improvement project. It can work to the core of just about every organization.

Six Sigma is about continuous process improvement. The name Six Sigma comes from the calculations that show us how close we are to meeting our customer's requirements (the only real measurement that matters.) When we meet our customer's requirements 100%, we have zero deviation from our goal. Since Sigma is the Greek symbol for a standard deviation, we use Sigma to describe how close we are to meeting our customer's goals. The more Sigma, the closer we are to perfection. Six Sigma indicates we have met our goals with 99.99966% accuracy. Six Sigma also equates to 3.4 defect per 1 million products produced. That is close to perfection. Is our goal in training, perfection? Sure, why not? We can strive for perfection, even if we know it can't be achieved. When Jack Welch introduced Six Sigma to GE, he stated "We are going to shift the paradigm from fixing products to fixing and developing processes, so we are producing nothing but perfection or close to it." When I look at a quote from one of the best business minds of our time, I learn that there is nothing wrong with having a lofty goal. The question remains: what does Six Sigma have to do with training? I believe the act of training is a process with a product. When I talk about what a trainer produces. I am not referring to the widget that they are training on, but rather the training itself' a trainer produces customer service of sorts. Six Sigma is perfect for services organizations. If you ask me (and by reading this you are), training (customer service) is a process that can be measured and improved.

Tesla Teaching

As I stated before, Six Sigma is about process improvement and training is a process. Six Sigma is about improving speed, quality, and complexity. Speed, quality and complexity are paramount to training (and just about every other service related business) success and therefore the process of training (and other service businesses) is an example one that is optimal for Six Sigma improvement.

So, let's take the DMAIC process and apply it to training in some way. This is just an example of a way to use the DMAIC process to improve training. You can use this to build your own way to improve your training in some way. The bottom line is that you are committed to quality and improving your training.

		Training Program Phase			
		Target Learning Objective Development	Single Minded Proposition	Understanding of Students	Tools Delivery Content
DMAIC Method	Define				
	Measure				
	Analyze				
	Improve				
	Control				

Figure 16

One way to ensure quality in your training is to build a checklist on what you have determined what a quality training is and to work to perform to that checklist. As is in sales, a lot of people complete a training session and determine that the training went well based on not having a metrics. Below is an example of a checklist you could use to base yours on to build a checklist for successful trainings.

Tesla Teaching

How you make training "good" is limited only by your imagination. Regardless of how you deliver it—group, coaching or mentoring, self-study, distance learning, webinar, video-conference, or other method, all good programs have certain elements in common—including:

- Clearly stated objectives. These are Target Learning Objectives. These establish participant expectations and focus trainers on what they need to accomplish.
- Good understanding of your audience. Different audiences can have different needs for the same information and will make different uses of it.
- Participant engagement. Especially important in adult education because adults bring experience or knowledge that traditional "students" may not. They want to contribute as well as take away—and they will look for ways to use what they learn. Engagement won't just happen. The leader has to create it.
- Good information. Application-based content that is accurate, relevant, and timely. It's not necessary that the participant know everything the trainer knows. Usually, some key points will do it. That is why you distinguish "need to know" from "nice to know."

- Good tools. These come in many forms, but the best trainers will use:
    o Leader Notes or Guides—to keep focused, on message and in sequence. Also, to create uniformity over multiple presentations.
    o Audio-visual support. People retain more when they see it and hear it. They learn most when they see it, hear it, and do it.
    o Lesson Plans—to keep the trainer on time and on track. And make changes "on the fly" when required.
    o Take-away materials. Participants use what they've learned after they leave. Good takeaways reinforce, remind, and allow for future reference.
    o Trainer checklists. Don't let a great program fail because no one remembered the extension cord or white board markers.
    o Test and measurement. To make sure material was learned
    o Good delivery. There are no dull subjects, there are only dull speakers.
    o Evaluation. This is important to measuring and improving performance

Another useful checklist to ensure quality is to have checkpoints prior to training, throughout training, and post training. Even a pilot with thousands of hours logged in the air uses a pre-flight and post-flight checklist: / every flight, every time. Why should trainers be any different? The main purpose of a checklist is to thwart the Foul-up Fairy. Don't let silly administrative oversights wreck a good program or steal class time while you look for the right connector.

Tesla Teaching

You can also send your checklist to people helping you with your program—such as the site coordinator at the meeting location or a co-presenter.

Following is an example of what we mean. You may want to create your own.

Date: _____   Times: _____
Group: _____
Location_____
Number of people expected: _____
Sponsor: _____
Cell: _____
email: _____

Pre-Meeting Tasks: Presenter
___Create/send agenda
___Send/confirm details with host
___Speaker introduction
___Email confirm w/agenda/instructions to: _____
___Name tags/table tents
___Assemble Handouts/takeaways
___Speaker evaluations
___Equipment
        (signage, posters, easel/pads, extension cord, projector,
                screen, power strips, recorder, other)
___Supplies (markers, tape, paper, batteries)
___Other_____
Pre-Meeting Tasks: Host
___Confirm places, times, AV, food with host
        (host admin/contact: _____)

Post-Meeting: Presenter
___Collect evals   __Sweep room ___   Thanks host
___Fulfill any commitments you made
___Settle expense matters
___Other_____

Lastly an important part of the quality program has to do with the PLAN-DO-CHECK process. The CHECK portion of this process can include a post training survey where the students provide feedback about the training. This is an important aspect of improving your training systems. As a trainer, you have to be able to have thick skin and to be able to take constructive criticism. This was one of the hardest aspects of training. People have opinions and adults will share them and sometimes they are not the nicest communicators when they are providing feedback about training. It is very important to take the feedback strictly as a way to improve. Below you will find a way to build your survey:

SESSION TITLE: ______________________________

PRESENTER: ____________________ FROM: KRAMER ELECTRONICS

DATE: ____________ LOCATION: ____________________

Please indicate your role:

☐ Architect ☐ Intern ☐ Specification Writer ☐ Legal/Accounting/Staff

☐ Sales ☐ Design ☐ Install ☐ Other

Certification/Member: NSCA and ESPA: ☐C-EST ☐EST (L2) InfoComm: ☐CTS - General/☐ CTS-Install/☐ CTS-Design

☐ AIA USGBC: ☐LEED-AP ☐ Other________

CIRCLE ONE NUMBER PER QUESTION:

	Poor/Disagree	......	...	Excellent/	Strongly	Agree
1. Overall satisfaction with this session:	1	2	3	4	5	6
2. Satisfaction with the *format* of this workshop:	1	2	3	4	5	6
3. Met overall personal objectives for attending:	1	2	3	4	5	6
4. Overall quality of training aids (handouts, audio/visual, etc):	1	2	3	4	5	6
5. Quality of session content and instruction:	1	2	3	4	5	6
6. The instructor was able to clearly communicate the subjects:	1	2	3	4	5	6
7. The instructor expressed interest in my learning the material:	1	2	3	4	5	6
8. The instructor presented the material in a logical manner:	1	2	3	4	5	6
9. Instructor demonstrated appropriate knowledge of material:	1	2	3	4	5	6
10. I would take another course taught by this instructor:	1	2	3	4	5	6
11. Applicability/value of new knowledge, ideas, or information:	1	2	3	4	5	6

How could this session be improved? ______________________________

____

What other topics would be of interest? ______________________________

Which training would you be most interested in next (circle one): AV/IT Green AV Sales

Applications Product General AV Technology Design Install Certification prep

Figure 17

Here are some key points to how to build your survey:
1. Use many points in the scale so that the person providing feedback can give at least a grade scale that resembles A-F like in school.
2. Use even numbers in your scale so that the reviewer does not just go down the middle, make them rate you and not just make it easy to stay noncommittal.
3. Use agree and disagree or poor and excellent statements and use high scores as good and low scores as bad. This is what people are used to seeing. Try not to switch this up – it will confuse people.
4. DO NOT tie the survey to course completing. It is tempting to make the survey a requirement. You should make the survey optional and only get surveys from people who WANT to provide it. Required surveys have little value.
5. Immediate feedback doesn't have as much value as feedback that comes about a week later. It is best to get feedback immediately after the course AND about a week after the course. This will help you determine how well the course did at helping information to stick.

CHAPTER 6

Confidence

Have an Attitude That Everyone Wants

(Knowledge is NOT Everything, Be Someone That Your
Attendees Will Want to Emulate – BE A MODEL)

"Fights between individuals, as well as governments and nations, invariably result from misunderstandings in the broadest interpretation of this term. Misunderstandings are always caused by the inability of appreciating one another's point of view."

– Nikola Tesla –
The Transmission of Electrical Energy Without Wires as a
Means for Furthering Peace, in Electrical World and Engineer
(January 7, 1905)

Tesla Teaching

Tesla Example – "Not only did he teach by accomplishment" Maj. Edwin H. Armstrong (who later won fame for his contributions for radio) "but he taught by inspiration of marvelous imagination that refused to accept the performance of what appeared to others to be insurmountable difficulties: an imagination the goals of which in a number of instances, are still in the realms of speculation." Nikola is not only self-confident but also shows confidence in others. The confidence Nikola shows in others inspires them. In a training environment this would inspire others to learn.

The Lesson – I love this example stated by Maj. Armstrong where he shows us an example that Nikola taught from a place of inspiration. The statement refers to Tesla's refusal to accept the performance of other's insurmountable difficulties. As instructors, teachers, trainers, and facilitators we should aspire to do nothing, but to inspire people to learn. I may not be able to teach people all that I need to teach them but if I can inspire them to learn what they can; I have done so much more.

If you think about this concept in deeper terms: think about someone's potential. How much can you impact their potential by teaching them a subject by how much you know that subject rather than inspiring them to learn about that same subject? If you have inspired them to learn, you have encouraged all methods of learning and not just the information you can provide. As a trainer, I wish to inspire learning and not just teach.

Tesla Teaching

So now the question becomes what does it take to inspire your students to learn? How can we, as trainers, inspire that kind of confidence? Here are 5 ways to help improve student's confidence:

1. Help them prepare (over prepare) – supply lots of reinforcement materials.

   Nothing builds confidence more than being the "smartest" guy in the room. The truth is, nine times out of 10, the "smartest" guy in the room is really the most prepared. Let them know that and ensure they do their homework by role playing the scenarios they're most likely to face. The next time it will be easier. To enforce this, I usually use flash cards and a lot of repetition.

2. Celebrate incremental improvements – use lots of quizzes and testing – make sure they are set to pass these tests.

   Have you ever tried confidence bursts? They're like running or training bursts, followed by a period of "active recovery." You can build more confidence and competence on your classes by training them in intervals and testing them and making sure they can win/pass. It is not the grueling hours but the constant pushing on limits and stretching of competence levels that leads to growth. Confidence is built through wins.

3. Have them teach others – teach back is one of the best ways to ensure confidence.

   Take note of their very best skills and gifts, and have them share with others in the class. If they know they're good at something specific, they'll be more apt to have the confidence to help teach it. If they resist, maybe have them do it in smaller groups. Then have them be participants in other trainings who are doing the same. This will have them build confidence in what they know and learn more about what they aren't strong in.

4. Encourage them through mistakes – if people can make mistakes in a safe environment, they can use these mistakes to build confidence.

   When a student lacks confidence, even the smallest mistake will affirm their feelings of inadequacy. Help students realize that failure is indeed a step to success. Teach them to "fail forward," to make the most of their mistakes.

5. Make sure they know that you and many others have been in their shoes – whether the training is for a certification or some other level.

   When the student knows that they are in the same place as others you have trained, or where even you have been, they are likely to be more confident. You can raise their confidence by easing their fears that you have trained people in their position before and that you too have been there as well.

Building confidence takes time and energy. It's worth it. It creates long-term impact for the student. Turning around confidence will rank high on your personal lifetime training achievement awards. No one will call it out, but you'll know and so will they. This is the difference between teaching someone something and inspiring them to learn.

An additional section on facilitation to build confidence in adult learners

Since one of the ways to inspire confidence is to have the students who are strong in a particular subject help teach it, it is important to spend a little more time covering some facilitation techniques.

Tesla Teaching

Before we cover facilitation, it is important to cover what adult learners are looking for when they came to training:

1. What do you need to know about adult learners to engage them in a facilitated session best? Adults have a need to know why they should learn something before they'll invest time in a learning event. As trainers, we must ensure that the learners know the purpose for training as early as possible. Participants need to know how this information or content is going to affect them and how it will make a difference.

2. They have a self-concept of who they are. Adults enter any learning situation seeing themselves as self-directing, responsible grown-ups and they don't like taking direction from others. Therefore, trainers must help adults identify their needs and direct their own learning experience. The students will establish their own goals.

3. They bring life experience and want to be recognized. Adults come to a learning opportunity with a wealth of experience and a great deal to contribute. Trainers will be more successful if they identify ways to build on and make use of adults' hard-earned knowledge, skill, and experience.

4. They prefer relevance. Adults have a strong readiness to learn those things that they can apply to their daily work. Training that relates directly to situations adults' hard-earned experience and knowledge.

5. They are practical. Adults are willing to devote energy to learning those things that they believe will help them perform well or solve problems. Trainers who determine needs and interests and develop content in response to those needs will be most helpful to adult learners.

6. They are internally motivated. Adults are more responsive to internal motivators, such as increased self-esteem, than they are to external motivators, such as higher salaries. Trainers can ensure that this is internal motivation is not blocked by barriers.

Tesla Teaching

When teaching courses to adult learners, it is important to remember that the class may have many students that have a similar level of knowledge, skill, and experience as you, possibly more. This may be a key reason to approach your adult learning in a facilitated session manner. Your responsibility is to draw out their skills, knowledge, and experience and have them share it with the entire class so that everyone can benefit from them.

Your confidence will be higher when you can deal with all the different types of attendees. Below you will find a list of the categories of attendees and ways to deal with them. Every adult learner can contribute to your course; your job is to take their knowledge, skill, and attitude along with their character and to make it work for you to truly contribute to the class environment.

Participant Chrematistic	Recommendation
Talkative Tom (the over performer who dominates)	Encourage initially. Turn their comments back at the group. Avoid eye contact. Don't recognize.
Silent Sue (says nothing or one-word answers)	Ask easy, open questions. Reinforce when she does speak up. Seat next to Talkative Tom.
Off-base Ozzie (either badly wrong or off on tangents)	Be gentle. Take responsibility for the sidetracking. Say "thanks" and return to the subject at hand.
Griping Gertrude (negative, complainer)	Ask for positive alternative. Turn her over to the group. Ignore her.

Tesla Teaching

Participant Characteristics	Recommendation
Whispering Wes (side conversations)	Ask to repeat for all to hear. Ask him for a comment on the last remark. Stop and wait. Move closer.
Argumentized Alice (takes exception to every point)	Stay calm. Don't engage her. Agree when you can, give her to the group when you can't.
Rambling Ron (has a lot to say and says it all)	Hear him out once. Later, interrupt at any pause. Summarize succinctly. Ask him to condense.
Heckling Hester (the comic sniper)	Thank her for her humor. Don't take her on (she's had a lot of practice at this.) Suggest serious alternatives or request she do so.
Obnoxious Oscar (personality clash with you or another group member)	Seat a maximum distance from the antagonist. Direct his attention to the objectives/subject at hand.

Figure 18

Tesla Teaching

CHAPTER 7

Controversy

Make Everyone Want to Take Action

(Provide Your Audience with a Call to Action and a
Compelling Reason to Act)

*"Let the future tell the truth, and evaluate each
one according to his work and accomplishments.
The present is theirs; the future, for which I have
really worked, is mine."*
– Nikola Tesla –
A Visit to Nikola Tesla, by Dragislav L. Petkoviæ in Politika
(April 1927)

Tesla Teaching

Tesla Example – When Nikola would demonstrate high voltage, he would sit and read in a cage with bolts of "lightning" scattering all around him. The show was both impressive and frightening at the same time. He would use this spectacle to engage the audience so they would learn about AC. What they were once afraid of, they now took the time to learn about. In this "training," Nikola would have his audience choose a side of a very controversial subject and then learn more about that subject.

The Lesson – Tesla would use his ability to communicate on almost every level to get people to engage and then commit to a side of a controversial subject. With that commitment, they learned. With our training, we can assign our subject to some controversy and get a commitment so that people learn better. The lesson here is controversy = training that sticks. Not only did Nikola challenge the normal and status quo, he set goals for people that were considered a huge challenge for the individual to accept. That is what this chapter is about. When we train, present or collaborate/communicate, we need to ask our students or audience and peers to act after the event. When there is a call to action, people tend to own the information and commit to it.

When you are training, it is important to engage early and immediately head toward the goal. A lot of trainers tend to make introductions and spend time thanking their hosts and such. It is more important that you engage the audience and start the training. The introductions can come in time. It is best to first set the hook:
- Tell a story that:
  - Satisfies the "what's in it for me?" question early
  - Forces the audience to take a position and to start to think or believe in something (Chapter 7)
    - Personal conviction

- Being believable
- Telling the truth
- Providing value

In the above points, the important one to focus on regarding this section is having the students think deeply, take a position on a subject, and engage their personal conviction. When students engage on this level they learn more. Emotion combined with logical thinking will make the subject sink in more strongly. A little stress and emotional tie in will embed the lesson deeper than just facts alone.

The controversy could be as simple as a challenge you issue at the beginning of the course. For example: you could say "Today I am going to have you look at a subject in a whole new way. I challenge you to look at (Insert Subject Here) in new light." Of course, you have to deliver on this challenge. This would require that you present your content in a manner that makes people think a little different.

Another way to get your students to embrace the controversy side of the training is to facilitate the controversy. If you know the major positions in a given subject, you can facilitate a discussion amongst the class groups that focus on these positions. This does require the facilitator's ability to guide the conversations towards the conclusion that your content needs them to come to.

In the AV industry, there are some controversies that I can use as examples to illustrate these types of discussions. For example, a lot of people love to discuss HDBaseT versus AVoverIP. Both are valid technologies and require a lot of training to implement. A good facilitator can use the controversy to have the students take a side and engage in a meaningful discussing during the course. This will help to assign emotion and buy-in during the training. Ultimately the discussion will have the students owning the content because they will be part of creating that content. You, as a facilitator, will have fulfilled their need to contribute and be treated as a peer. Another win-win. It is important that you focus on your duty to guide the conversation to meet your Target Learning Objectives (TLOs).

When you are working with controversial material and people are placed where they need to take a side (which I have clearly encouraged due to it being a way that people lock content away in their brains), there are some steps you can take to help them learn the content even when they are not willing to change their position on the subject. It is important that you are not necessarily looking to change their position but rather you are trying to help them to learn a subject (or more importantly, be inspired to learn a subject) by assigning that subject to a controversial position as well. But you do not need to change their mind. Here are some steps you can take to help them learn the subject without trying to change their position on a controversial matter:

- Lay a foundation of trust, be authentic, and consistent.
- Maintain a positive classroom setting.
- Listen, listen, listen – ask questions and listen some more.
- Demonstrate the benefits of changing.
- Use visuals and graphics to make the point.
- Design experiential learning activities, allowing enough time to process what happened, determine what it means, and identify what learners will do differently as a result.
- Use role plays, especially reserved roles to explore positions from different perspectives. This could even just be writing notes from the other perspectives.
- Conduct self-assessments to help participants understand their priorities or values.
- Encourage journaling and schedule reflection time. This could be in the form of notes about what they learn about each position and discussion about this at later times.
- Allow for time to "digest" the content and discuss it in groups in later sessions.

Tesla Teaching

One thing about controversy is that stress can be a positive part of training. In some cases, I have seen trainers try to create a completely stress-free training environment. This too is a controversial subject. You need to add a little controversy into your training by adding a little stress. Challenge your students and stress them a little. The stress will also help to log in some of the content. The stress engages different part of the brain and the more different parts you can engage the more likely it is that things will stay with the learner. So, give a few difficult tests, or do some timed hands-on challenges or competitions. Add a little stress and it will go a long way.

Another thing about controversy is that you should not be too concerned talking about controversial subjects because audiences want you to succeed. If you have anxiety about speaking about certain subjects you should consider the following about speaker anxiety.

Developing good delivery technique includes confronting speaker anxiety. Almost everyone—including professional speakers and trainers—experiences some anxiety before a speech or a training course. This is real, not imaginary. And it's far more good than bad.

When 3,000 people were asked what they were afraid of, 41% mentioned speaking before a group—making it the number 1 most common human fear! Only 19% mentioned death—making it number 7 on the same list. (That doesn't make speaker anxiety the worst human fear, only the most common one.)

Tesla Teaching

Here are few things the pros have learned that may put this in perspective:

- Audiences don't attack. Generally, they are supportive and helpful. They want you to succeed. After all, they invested their time to come hear what you had to say. How would it be in their self-interest to see you fail? Remember that the audience doesn't actually know what you intended to do or say—and they can't judge you at all on anything you didn't do, so unless you call attention to something, they'll just play along!
- Preparation is your best defense against anxiety. Much anxiety comes from the possibility that something will go wrong. Thorough preparation not only reduces the number of things that could go wrong, it helps you handle the ones that do.
- Be yourself. Don't be concerned that you aren't tall, funny, handsome, polished—or like someone else you saw that looked successful. Most presenters are average everyday people, not show biz personalities. Trying to be like someone else takes energy away from being a good "you". It usually fails anyway. Forget it.
- Anxiety is normal and good. Keeps you on your game—just like an athlete has pre-game jitters.
- Anxiety is physical. Under stress, you may have a faster heart rate, dry mouth, physical shakes or other symptoms. This is adrenalin doing what adrenalin does.
- Anxiety is social. No one wants to make a mistake or "look bad" to others. But you are no more likely to make a mistake here than in driving a car, grilling a steak, or buying a suit. If you play golf, you know exactly what we mean!
- Anxiety is psychological. Some people erect barriers to their own success—call it self-limiting beliefs. You increase your chances of "looking bad" if you believe you will.

-

CHAPTER 8

Bonus - Creativity

Acting Without Being Given Direction

(Help Your Audience to Learn to Act Without Direction)

"I do not think there is any thrill that can go through the human heart like that felt by the inventor as he sees some creation of the brain unfolding to success... such emotions make a man forget food, sleep, friends, love, everything."
– Nikola Tesla –
In Cleveland Moffitt, "A Talk With Tesla", Atlanta Constitution (7 Jun 1896)

Tesla Example – Tesla had the ability to envision his creations/inventions in his mind with incredible detail. He was able to design, build, prototype, test and operate his inventions in his mind. With this ability, he could see if his invention wouldn't work and he would go back to design in his head without ever actually going to physical design. This was a great example of his incredible imagination and his ability to use it. He used this imagination to engage his creativity.

The Lesson – Tesla teaches us that we can use our imagination and rehearse in our minds as well as in front of a mirror. We can also walk through what may work and what may not work. We can also learn that we should do what works for us. Tesla used his methods even though Edison had other methods to market that clearly seemed quicker and better proven. Tesla stuck to what worked for him and used his creative methods.

In this section, you will see the creative methods that I use to make my training unique.

Max's Tips – Straight from the field

These are some techniques that I have developed over time. I am not here to say that I am an expert by any means. I am saying that everyone has the ability to add their own value and unique skills to the equation. In this section, I would like to share what little things I do differently to make my trainings special.

The Opening

This sub-section discusses how to take certain weaknesses that I have and how I use them to make them strengths

Make a personal connection

Later in this section I discuss how I use tent cards and how I prefer to make introductions. I recommend that introductions be made a little later in the training so that people get to the meaning of the training first and understand why they are there and what is in it for them first. But when you do get into the introductions, I do believe it is important to make a connection to the students. This may be contrary to what many books say. I believe that training is a conversation and that to gain credibility and to show sincerity you need to truly engage your audience and to do this you need to connect. To do this, you need to take it to a personal level. Tell stories about kids and or family

I like to tell stories about my family and include ones about my kids. This helps the students to connect with me on a personal level. They know I am human and that I have a life outside of where I am now. The important thing here is to make these stories topical and to make sure they tie into the lesson in some meaningful way.

Set the environment / own the space
It is important to set a classroom space that allows for open communication and that is as intimate as it can be. We recently conducted a training that had lower attendance than was expected. Because attendance was low, we had much larger space and more tables and chairs than were needed. In order to make the space more conducive to open and

intimate communication, I removed a few of the tables and closed in the training space. This is counter intuitive, because, generally, people tend to think the more space I have. the better. But in training, it is better to have smaller space so that people are closer and feel more open to communicating with each other.

It is also important to set the stage for collaboration. This is tough to do when you are using rented spaces such as hotel conference centers and such, because they tend to not know how to set up collaborative spaces. "Rounds" are not really what we are looking for because we need to be able to go into presentation mode and collaboration mode. Using rounds doesn't allow for presentation mode because many of the students will have their back to the presentation. This may require a space that you can change the configuration on the fly. Be flexible.

Using a weakness as strength

This sub-section discusses how to take certain weaknesses I have and how I use them to turn them into strengths. I am not saying everyone should use these techniques exactly as stated, but rather to find ways to use their weaknesses and turn them into strengths. Stand back and look at what you may consider a weakness and look through the lens of "how can I take this and make it to where others can benefit from it?" You can often find that you can take many things you considered your weakness and allow people to gain from the way you work around them.

Tent Cards

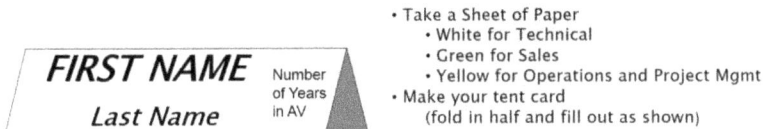

- Take a Sheet of Paper
  - White for Technical
  - Green for Sales
  - Yellow for Operations and Project Mgmt
- Make your tent card
  (fold in half and fill out as shown)

FIRST NAME Number of Years in AV
Last Name

Figure 19

Have students make name cards to place in front of them so that you can call them by name.

You can also use colored cards to identify the jobs that they do and add information about how long they have been in the business on the card.

I can have them put their contact information on the inside of the card as well. One unique added feature is that I have them put one thing about themselves that no one else in the room knows about them. Later in the class I can collect the cards and play a game where we try to guess who is assigned to that unique thing.

Tesla Teaching

Tesla Teaching

Why do I really use these tent cards? I have a really bad memory when it comes to connecting/remembering names and faces. To overcome this, this is one of the first activities I use in a training session utilized the tent cards. Break the class into small groups of 3-5 people and have these groups introduce themselves to each other.

The Introductions: I have these groups (of 3-5) introduce themselves to each other rather than to the larger class for few reasons. Think about it. When you are sitting in a class and the class is going through the classic introduction when every student introduces themselves to the entire class, do you really remember anyone's name? Chances are you are focusing on what you are going to say when it is your turn. The way I do introductions is to have smaller groups introduce themselves to each other, but make sure that they know that one of the people in that group is going to have to introduce their group to the rest of the class. You will be amazed at how the dynamics change now that everyone else in that smaller group knows that they need to be able to introduce their group to the rest of the class. They become better listeners and now know everyone's name and some details about the people in their group.

Another keynote about using this way of making introductions is the lesson in sales. The simple lesson about shut-up and listen is key. The people in the group are retaught the lesson that introductions are for the purpose of listening and gathering information.

Group Leaders

The other area that you can use a weakness as a strength is where you can use people in the class as group leaders. This is not necessarily because you are weak or managing large groups. I am actually pretty good at managing a lot of people. In some cases, it does not matter how good you are, it can come down to just being a bandwidth issue. In the managing a large class, you can assign group leaders to help facilitate gathering information from the groups and sharing the groups' consensus on answers.

A good facilitator can facilitate other facilitators. This takes a lot of practice but when done well, this can bring out new information that otherwise would not come out during traditional training sessions. Here are some of the keys to being a top facilitator and using group leaders instead of just presenting:

Appearance

This sub-section discusses how appearance can impact your training. There are so many opinions on how one should dress and how you should stand and act during training sessions. I only have a couple of hints that I care to share from my experience. I will share a couple of hints about how I stand and act and how I dress.

Tesla Teaching

Animated / Natural

When presenting, it is hard to keep the balance of being animated while still acting natural. A lot of trainers will go to one extreme or the other. My advice is to be conversational. Here is how I do this. There is always (okay, almost always) at least one person in your training session that you can consider a "friend" or "champion." It is easy to identify this person early on. They are typically in the front row or on the aisle. They arrive early and set up with lots of pens and paper, highlighters and are generally over prepared. They are your "cheerleader." You can use them as your base. When you start your training, start off as if you are having a conversation with them. Make sure you still scan the audience and make short but natural eye contact with several students but use your base person or people to have a natural conversation with. This will help you be animated but natural.

Overdress

My recommendation for how to dress is pretty simple. I usually where a suit and tie to my trainings. I know in today's business world a suit and tie is overkill. I have consciously decided to always overdress because it is always easier to dress down than to try to dress up. This can also send a message. When I was in a training a couple months ago, I started with the whole suit and tie and went for a half-hour or so. Then I said, "you guys seem like a great group and like you get along really well. Do you mind if I dress down a little bit and get down to business with you?" With that, I set the stage that I was willing to join them. I used the dress statement to ask if I could "join" their team. And with that, they consciously invited me to be part of them for the day. There is a sales aspect to training and a facilitator can work this part into their training.

Add Character

It is really helpful to add some character to your training. The people in your training could have read a book or whitepaper or they could have taken an online training. Instead they took your class. In a previous chapter I mention "the you" factor. If "the you" factor is humor then give them what they came for.

Self-Deprecate

We have already established that training takes humility. In this case it helps to be able to make fun of yourself. In many training sessions, the group is well established and you can rarely make fun of anyone in the room without the whole room turning on you. But people love a good roast so the best solution: make fun of yourself. Students will love the fact that you don't take yourself too seriously. Unless you are a college professor and have a few PhDs after your name, you are likely not the smartest person in the room anyway. I like to say that if I am the smartest person in the room, then this is going to be a boring class. So, lighten up and have some fun, even at your own expense.

Entertain

I am not bragging, but I was awarded the Educator of the Year award in 2010 by InfoComm. The reason I tell you this is because my friends and fellow educators refer to this as the Edutainer of the Year award. Whether you use humor, or whatever your strength is, you can entertain. Use that "you" factor to entertain your students. One example is I have one fellow instructor that is not very funny at all, but he is one of the most intelligent people I know. He can entertain a group by telling them facts and sharing stories about some of the most incredible projects he has worked on. His dry humor is a little entertaining, but he knows his strength is in being himself and entertaining the group through knowledge.

Using Visuals

I am not telling you that you should trick your students, but this is just a little hint on how to impress students and how to keep them engaged. The first is for when you are still using flip charts and the other is just when you are just standing in front of any room.

Pencils for hidden notes

When you are using flipcharts, it is really hard to write neat or to make really nice circles or other drawings clearly. One technique that I have learned is to write the notes on the flipchart in pencil ahead of time. The students cannot see these notes from the distance that they are sitting at but when you trace them with the marker, it looks like you are writing them freehand. It is quite impressive when you can draw a complicated drawing on a flipchart freehand in the middle of class with near perfection.

Hands as visual aids

Sometimes it is helpful if you are able to make a model of what you are discussing with your hands. This is especially true if you can have the students do the same. This way, the students can take the model with them wherever they go. Use this same modeling method with as many of the visuals in the course as you can. This helps to engage your audience and keep your value in the equation. It is important that the visuals are part of the learning, that they make sense, and they support the content in a meaningful way. If you can use your hands to do all of this it is very helpful.

Managing the Audience

In this section, I will cover different ways that I use to manage the audience and the learning environment. These are techniques that I use and I recommend putting your own touch on them that make them natural to you.

Adults and tactile learning

Adults are tactile and they learn more when they have items in their hands and when they can assign content to tactile connections. For example, if an adult learner can touch a physical model of something or even build with Lego building blocks or use Play-Doh while they are learning a subject, they are engaging a portion of their brain that assigns the subject to a separate part of their memory. My hint from the field is to also make this part memorable by using something memorable. I found little rubber body parts at Wal-Mart that stretch and bend. The student can touch and bend these while listening to a subject. They are also weird and make things memorable in their own weird way. Some instructors use scented markers and other items that engage other senses.

Borrow authority

This technique can be used when you are not the Subject Matter Expert. You can research and have others teach you the content in a manner that makes you feel completely comfortable enough to teach it yourself. You can have product managers teach you content or have certified trainers teach you a technology. Then, when it comes time to teach, you simply state, "I have been taught by the industry's best and most talented in (INSERT TOPIC HERE) and they provided me with the content here to share with you." This is borrowed authority. This way you can make it clear that you are passing on information that was given to you by THE authority in the subject.

110

Tesla Teaching

Use diffusing phrases – "Did I explain that okay?"

One of the most important techniques I have developed over time is how I learned to take the responsibility of understanding upon myself. A lot of instructors will ask if their students understand a subject This implies that it is the student's fault if they do not understand. I have learned to ask, "Did I explain that okay?" This allows the students to ask me to explain it a different way. The problem is my own, not theirs. They can say "No, you did not explain that okay." It then becomes my responsibility to explain it in the way they are comfortable. After all, that is what is important. What I say in training is not what is important; what is heard is important.

Make people correct and guide their comments without dominating

It is important that students feel comfortable enough to contribute in training sessions. I have found that a simple turn of phrase helps to make this happen. When I have someone that wants to engage and they don't have the concept quite right, if I take the time to find a small portion of what they said to be correct and build on that, it works better than to say wrong and start from scratch. For example, if a student were to make the statement that a car runs on air. Rather than to say no it runs on gasoline or diesel, I could say that the fuel is gasoline or diesel but for that to burn, it requires oxygen. You are correct. The combination of both is required. The more correct answer for a quiz or test would be gasoline or diesel. This way, they can be correct and then you can guide their comments and use them to teach the lesson as intended by the Target Learning Objectives (TLOs) defined.

Make it memorable

This is probably one of my favorite areas of training. Really this comes down to just making the training yours. I have trained a few trainers and one thing I can caution you about is to not try to emulate another trainer. I have observed a couple of trainers try to conduct my training exactly how I train and that resulted in a train wreck. I will not go into details, but it was ugly. Here is an example of a couple of the things I do to add to my training to make it a little more memorable.

2,4,6,8...

This is a portion of the training where the students are calculating the farthest viewer from an image based on the task that the viewer is performing. The rule is that for detail viewing you would multiply the image heights by 4, for general tasks multiply by 6 and for videos you multiply by 8. The rule for closest viewer is also that the closest viewer should be no closer than 2 times the height of the image. So, when I teach this, I have the students sing 2, 4, 6, 8 who do we appreciate - Max, Max, Max. Then we make the joke that they will never forget this. As hard as they will try to forget, they will never forget this. Memorable? I think so.

The Max Dance

Another memorable thing that I add to my training is whenever I must add an element to the training that sounds salesy or cheesy, I do a little tap dance. After class, I have heard as this referred to as 'The Max Dance.' People remember this and the content for years after the class. The point is to make your course memorable in some way- your way.

Another important factor is to set your own criteria for what makes a "good training." You cannot perform to a metric without setting that metric. If you looked back at the last training and asked yourself "How did that training, go?" can you answer that question specifically against measurable criteria or do you just go against a gut feel? Here is an outline of some ideas of how you can set your criteria for "good training."

The Big 5:
1. Clearly Stated Objectives
2. Understanding of Audience
3. Engagement
4. Content / Applicable Information
5. Using Presentation Notes / Leader's Guide

Let's breakdown each of the Big 5 items in more detail:

Clearly Stated Objectives

These were referred to in chapter 2 and establish participant expectations and focus the trainer on needs to be accomplished. After the training is complete the trainer should take another look at these objectives and see if they were properly set and how this played out in the actual class. This falls completely in line with the time, scope, and cost as well as the mission, values, and vision.

This also emphasizes the importance of the planning phase of training project management and then the PLAN-DO-CHECK approach (cycle) where you recheck how your plan worked.

Having a plan doesn't mean that you are locked in to what you are doing and can never get to do what you are truly passionate about. Your plan can have options and different paths to take at different times depending on all kinds of factors. The idea of the strategic plan is to know where you ultimately want to be and to make sure your execution and tactical plans include a means to get to that goal. This also doesn't mean that everything has to work toward that goal. There will always be distracters and events that take place that derail your plans. A great plan includes contingency actions for just that reason. There is a very helpful method taught in many project management and process improvement circles that includes a PLAN, DO, CHECK process. This way your plan is dynamic. When you check, you may find that you need to re-plan. It is a continuous process.

When we look at how the Plan-Do-Check model works for Tesla Teaching we also add in the Train portion. This makes perfect sense because our ultimate plan is to train and be successful and the 7 keys to Tesla Teaching should result in better training and communication success. Everything else hinges on this plan. The beauty is that the plan is an iterative process that one can revisit throughout their career and adjust to improve and make proper adjustments as needed.

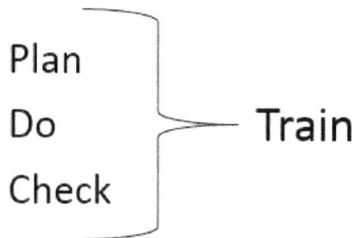

Plan
Do   — Train
Check

Figure 20

Tesla Teaching

Content / Applicable Information

Obviously, the information you provide should be complete, current, and timely. But here are some other considerations in what constitutes "appropriate" information:

There should not be too much of it. Good planning and practice will tell you how much time you need to cover a subject. Cramming material in leads to confusion and overload. If you have an hour—and you plan to have some interchange—put 45 to 50 minutes of material in. Better to add something unintended if you have extra time than to leave out something important if you run short.

Make sure it's logically sequenced and neat. Move from the general to the specific. Use examples and anecdotes to put information into a context the group can relate to.

Get material edited by someone other than the original writer. Even the best writers do this and it always improves the finished product.

If you want to include material you don't intend to cover in the training, it's OK to put it in the take-away package, but tell your group it's there for reference and you didn't intend to cover it. Don't leave them to wonder why you "didn't get to it." Sometimes this works best as an appendix.

Use visuals at every opportunity. A picture really can be worth a thousand words.

Do not let your passion or your personal expertise get the better of you. If you know 100 things about your subject, pick the half-dozen this group this group needs to know.

Using Presentation Notes / Leader's Guide

You should always work from some form of Leader's Guide. Here are some choices:

PowerPoint 3-to-a-page handouts view with notes in the margin associated with each slide, even if the slide is a blank.

PowerPoint Notes page. This is the format Microsoft seems to recommend, but it has its pros and cons. It's helpful if you need more notes to go with your slide, but it only works well if all the information you need fits on the page.

Simple bullet-point outline of your own design with marginal notes to yourself. Seasoned trainers use this format a lot. (e.g. HAND OUT WORKBOOKS NOW or GOOD TIME FOR A BREAK? or HAVE GROUPS OFFER THEIR OWN EXAMPLES HERE.] It helps to have notes to yourself be in ALL CAPS because you are not meant to speak them aloud. The human eye is accustomed to follow upper and lowercase text—so when you use ALL CAPS it attracts special attention from you and reminds you not to say it aloud.

Feel free to use your own "cues" in your tools but be sure to be consistent so you do not get confused. You can use a special cue [i.e., *] to signify it is time to advance the slide.

Full narrative text. This has the advantage of uniformity when multiple presenters are conducting the same training, when you are working with material someone else prepared, or when you are not expert in the subject. I suggest this be done in a separate document since full lesson plan development should be done outside of PowerPoint anyway. This also has the disadvantage of temptation to "read it like a speech"—which hurts spontaneity, eye contact, and engagement.

It is not recommended to use index cards or loose-leaf pages, simply because they can too easily get out of sequence. If you choose to use these, make sure that they are numbered!

Lastly – The one thought I want to leave you with is one I mentioned earlier. Are you training people so that they learn your content or are you trying to inspire them to learn about your content? The difference is considerable. The difference is what makes you Train Like Niko.

Tesla Teaching

Closing Thoughts

"It's about having passion and purpose then worrying about profit." – Max Kopsho

Bibliography and Recommended Reading

Biech, Elaine (2017). The Art and Science of Training. ASTD DBA the Association for Talent Development (ATD).

Cheney, Margaret (1981). Tesla, Man Out of Time. Touchstone – Simon & Schuster.

Filiquarian Publishing, LLC (2007). The Problem of Increasing Human Energy. Nikola Tesla. Filiquarian Publishing, LLC.

Max Kopsho (2016). The Art and Science of Da Vince Sales – The Seven Keys to Selling Like Leonardo – grAVITation TECHnologies.

Neil Rackham, Neil (1988). SPIN Selling. McGraw Hill, Inc.

Page, Rick. (2002). Hope is Not a Strategy - The 6 Keys to Winning the Complex Sale. McGraw Hill.

Performance Research Associates, Inc. (2003). *Delivering Knock Your Socks Off Service*

SoHo Books (2012). My Inventions, The Autobiography of Nikola Tesla. SoHo Books.

About the Author

Max has 32 years of training and communications/collaboration in the unified communications industry and is partner/owner of one of the industry's top consulting firms for sales training and sales process improvement. He carries some of the top certifications in networking and audiovisual technologies. Max has been the keynote speaker for several industry events and was awarded InfoComm's Educator of the Year Award in 2010. He has taught Tesla Teaching and Da Vinci Sales to tens of thousands of people in several organizations worldwide.

Max holds advanced certifications in project management, networking, network security, operational excellence, QA/QC and audiovisual design and installation. Max has achieved a great deal of success in network security, technology channel sales and channel/market development. He has been a senior academy faculty member for InfoComm University for over a decade. Max has developed and executed comprehensive global training programs for industry associations, channel partners and for technology manufacturers. His experience in Unified Communications includes videoconference and collaborative environment design for global enterprises, development, training and implementation. Max served in the U.S. Army for 10 years where he gained his initial experience in computer/electronics technology and worked with complex computer networks, advanced radar systems and specialized electronics and thermal and night vision imaging devices.

Max, his wife (Christine – a four-time cancer victor) and one (Joe – 18 (also at UGA)) of their four children live in Sugar Hill GA (their other children are Mike-31, Amanda-30 and Matt-26). Max and Christine also have a 12-year old grandson (Aaronn Jr.) and a 6month old grandson (Mattis). They spend their free time at boating, fishing, camping and supporting Leukemia and Lymphoma society events.

Table of Figures

Figure 1	Knowledge – Skill - Attitude
Figure 2	Technology, People, and Place
Figure 3	The 7 C's of Hierarchy of Communications
Figure 4	The Interdependent Growth of the 7 C's
Figure 5	Technology, People, and Place
Figure 6	Table of Technologies and Tools
Figure 7	SMILE Chart
Figure 8	The "You Factor"
Figure 9	Content and Capabilities Bridge
Figure 10	Example for Evaluating Presentation Skills
Figure 11	Sample Lesson Plan
Figure 12	The "You Factor" EngagEmEnt Connection
Figure 13	Tesla's Motorized Flying Disk
Figure 14	Vision, Mission, Principles
Figure 15	Time, Scope, Cost - Iron Triangle
Figure 16	Six Sigma - Training Improvement Program
Figure 17	Sample Post Training Survey
Figure 18	Dealing with Character Types in Training
Figure 19	Example Tent Card
Figure 20	Plan, Do, Check - Train

Some of the figures in this book are forms and may appear very small in the book. These forms and other resources for Tesla Teaching can be found at no cost at: www.gravitationtech.com/tesla-resources.

The Art and Science of
Tesla Teaching
The 7 Keys to Training Like Nikola

By: Max Kopsho

Tesla Teaching™

We hope you enjoyed the book. Please go to Amazon and review it and recommend it to others.

★ ★ ★ ★ ★

AVIXA
CTS (RU) Provider

www.gravitationtech.com/tesla-quiz

www.ingramcontent.com/pod-product-compliance
Lightning Source LLC
Chambersburg PA
CBHW071006040426
42443CB00007B/684